I0473958

U.S. Department of Justice
Office of Justice Programs
810 Seventh Street N.W.
Washington, DC 20531

Alberto R. Gonzales
Attorney General

Tracy A. Henke
Acting Assistant Attorney General

Sarah V. Hart
Director, National Institute of Justice

This and other publications and products of the National Institute
of Justice can be found at:

National Institute of Justice
www.ojp.usdoj.gov/nij

Office of Justice Programs
Partnerships for Safer Communities
www.ojp.usdoj.gov

JUNE 05

Mass Fatality Incidents: A Guide for Human Forensic Identification

Technical Working Group for Mass Fatality Forensic Identification

NCJ 199758

Sarah V. Hart
Director

Findings and conclusions of the research reported here are those of the authors and do not reflect the official position or policies of the U.S. Department of Justice.

The National Institute of Justice is a component of the Office of Justice Programs, which also includes the Bureau of Justice Assistance, the Bureau of Justice Statistics, the Office of Juvenile Justice and Delinquency Prevention, and the Office for Victims of Crime.

Message From the Director

Every action taken by public safety personnel at a death scene can have a profound impact on victim identification and any subsequent criminal investigation. Coordinating the work of the many agencies that must respond to mass fatality incidents presents a particularly complex set of demands. Even large States and municipalities can find themselves overburdened with many operational requirements in responding to a major transportation accident or terrorist incident. Whether for the purpose of preserving evidence for a criminal investigation or effectively managing the identification of victims, a well-designed plan could be an invaluable response tool.

Recent events and the emergent threat of continued terrorist activity emphasize the need for public-sector agencies to plan for a coordinated response to a mass fatality event. Agencies small and large, urban and rural, need to be prepared for an event that will exceed their operational capacity. In an effort to support excellence across local and State public safety agencies, the National Institute of Justice, the research, development, and evaluation arm of the U.S. Department of Justice, initiated a national effort through the National Center for Forensic Science to develop a consensus document that would offer guidance for the development of coordinated plans for responding to an incident involving mass fatalities. I commend the work of the 49 experienced public officials and other professionals from across the United States and Canada who came together and formed the Technical Working Group that developed this guide. I applaud their commitment and determination in creating this consensus document.

This guide is designed to assist all jurisdictions in creating new mass fatality plans or reviewing existing plans. I encourage every jurisdiction to give careful consideration to the recommendations in the guide. Regardless of the number of people killed, victims and their loved ones deserve our best efforts to provide accurate identification of the victims and effective investigation of the crime. I believe this guide will help us attain that goal.

Sarah V. Hart
Director, National Institute of Justice

Preface

Most government agencies concerned with public safety have disaster plans. Although some are linked to other agencies' plans, others are not. In the event of mass fatalities, the local medical examiner or coroner should already have in place a plan to identify the victims properly. The purpose of this guide is to help the medical examiner or coroner prepare that portion of a disaster plan concerned with victim identification.

The statutory duty of the medical examiner or coroner does not change as the number of victims increases. Whether there are one, a hundred, or thousands of victims, each should be accorded the same consideration under the laws governing the investigation of and response to sudden or violent death.

Correct victim identification is essential to satisfy humanitarian considerations, meet civil and criminal investigative needs, and identify victim perpetrators. Equally important with identification procedures is the need to document body location and wound patterns that may be essential in reconstructing the event and determining its cause. Today, forensic science (e.g., DNA, fingerprints, forensic anthropology, odontology, radiology) plays a major role in victim identification. If local and State governments lack the resources to cope with a large number of fatalities, they should consider outside help in the forensic investigations that may lead to the identification of these victims. The specialists brought in to assist in the investigation should have experience, education, and training in the forensic process and should adhere to the highest scientific and professional standards.

It is essential to integrate the medical examiner/coroner functions into the established emergency response system. This system is concerned with limiting the scope of the disaster and providing critical functions such as fire suppression, rescue of the injured, establishment of an incident command structure, and security. The first section of this guide, "Section 1: Initial Response Considerations," summarizes the initial process. The second section, "Section 2: Arriving at the Scene," discusses the integration of the medical examiner/coroner into the process. From the third section, "Section 3: Processing the Scene," onward, the focus is on the identification of the deceased.

This guide does not specifically address the search and rescue efforts for the living that take precedence over the recovery of the remains, collection of evidence, documentation of the scene, and other operational procedures. However, first responders and others can use this guide to understand the death investigation process. This guide can assist them in developing operational tactics for routine as well as mass fatality incidents.

The procedures presented in this guide can help medical examiners and coroners fulfill their legal duties even when the number of victims exceeds their agency's daily operating capacity.

Technical Working Group for Mass Fatality Forensic Identification

In April 2000, the National Institute of Justice (NIJ), the National Center for Forensic Science (NCFS), and the University of Central Florida identified the need for a guide to prepare local and State medical examiners and coroners for a mass fatality incident. NIJ established the Technical Working Group for Mass Fatality Forensic Identification (TWGMFFI) to identify, define, and establish the basic criteria to assist medical examiners' and coroners' offices and local and State agencies in managing mass fatality incidents.

The planning panel met in January and February 2001 at NCFS in Orlando, Florida, to define the scope, intent, and objectives of the guide and to identify TWG members and member organizations. NCFS facilitated the first meeting of the full TWGMFFI in June 2001 in Orlando, Florida. During the first day, the group separated into subcommittees to draft the following sections: "Section 1: Initial Response Considerations"; "Section 2: Arriving at the Scene"; "Section 3: Processing the Scene"; "Section 5: Disposition of Human Remains, Personal Effects, and Records"; and "Section 6: Other Issues." On the second day, the group separated into subcommittees according to their forensic specialties to draft "Section 4: Identification of Human Remains."

The planning panel was scheduled to meet in late September 2001 to review the draft document. The events of September 11, 2001, however, required NCFS to reschedule the meeting. The planning panel met in November 2001 in Orlando to review and edit the draft document. NCFS facilitated conference calls with each subcommittee during January through March 2002 to review and revise each section. NCFS hosted another planning panel meeting in Orlando in March 2002 to review and further revise the document. In May 2002, NCFS posted the draft document on its Web site and solicited comments from 335 agencies, departments, and organizations in the forensic science and law enforcement communities for content and editorial review. The full TWG met for the final time in July 2002 in Orlando to review comments, revise the document, and make final changes.

Planning Panel

Douglas M. Arendt
Captain, U.S. Navy (Retired)
Chief Forensic Odontologist and Staff
 Pathologist (Retired)
Armed Forces Institute of Pathology
Washington, D.C.

Jack Ballantyne, Ph.D.
Associate Director, Biological Evidence
National Center for Forensic Science
University of Central Florida
Orlando, Florida

Jamie Bush, CLPE
Forensic Scientist
Latent Print Section
Mississippi Crime Laboratory
Meridian, Mississippi

Frank A. Ciaccio, M.P.A.
Manager, Forensic Science
National Transportation Safety Board
Washington, D.C.

Joseph H. Davis, M.D.
Director (Retired)
Miami-Dade County Medical Examiner's
 Department
Miami, Florida

Joseph A. DiZinno, D.D.S.
Deputy Assistant Director
Laboratory Division
Federal Bureau of Investigation
Washington, D.C.

Anthony B. Falsetti, Ph.D.
Director
C.A. Pound Human Identification Lab
University of Florida
Gainesville, Florida

Mitchell M. Holland, Ph.D.
Vice President and Laboratory Director
The Bode Technology Group, Inc.
Springfield, Virginia

Thomas Holland, Ph.D.
Scientific Director
U.S. Army Central Identification
 Laboratory, Hawaii [now Joint POW/MIA
 Accounting Command]
Hickam AFB, Hawaii

Norman Kassoff
Director of Operations (Retired)
Miami-Dade County Medical Examiner's
 Department
Miami, Florida

William Morlang, D.D.S.
Colonel, U.S. Air Force (Retired)
Associate Professor
Department of Oral and Maxillofacial
 Pathology
Tufts University
Boston, Massachusetts

Tom Shepardson (Deceased)
DMORT National Commander
Office of Emergency Preparedness
National Disaster Medical System
U.S. Department of Health and Human
 Services [now U.S. Department of
 Homeland Security]
Syracuse, New York

Paul Sledzik, M.S.
DMORT III Commander
National Museum of Health and Medicine

Armed Forces Institute of Pathology
Washington, D.C.

Carrie M. Whitcomb, M.S.F.S.
Director
National Center for Forensic Science
University of Central Florida
Orlando, Florida

TWGMFFI Members

Joseph A. Bifano, M.D.
Major, U.S. Air Force
Chief, Diagnostic Imaging
Dover AFB, Delaware

C. Michael Bowers, D.D.S., J.D.
Deputy Medical Examiner
Ventura County Medical Examiner's Office
Ventura, California

Joseph Brown
Supervisory Fingerprint Specialist
Federal Bureau of Investigation
Washington, D.C.

Brian Chrz, D.D.S.
Consultant
Office of the Chief Medical Examiner
State of Oklahoma
Perry, Oklahoma

David Coffman
Crime Laboratory Analyst Supervisor
Florida Department of Law Enforcement
Tallahassee, Florida

Barry W. Duceman, Ph.D.
Director of Biological Science
Forensic Investigation Center
New York State Police
Albany, New York

Scott Firestone, D.D.S.
Forensic Odontologist
Suffolk County Medical Examiner's Office
Hauppauge, New York

John Fitzpatrick, M.D.
Department of Radiology

Cook County Hospital
Chicago, Illinois

Ron Fourney, Ph.D.
Research Scientist
Forensic Laboratory Services
National Police Services
Royal Canadian Mounted Police
Ottawa, Ontario
Canada

Diane France, Ph.D.
Director
Human Identification Laboratory
Colorado State University
Fort Collins, Colorado

Laura C. Fulginiti, Ph.D.
Forensic Anthropologist
Maricopa County Medical Examiner's
  Office
Phoenix, Arizona

Grant D. Graham, M.F.S.
Senior Crime Scene Analyst
Mississippi Crime Laboratory
Biloxi, Mississippi

Danny W. Greathouse
Lockheed Martin
U.S. Department of Justice
Washington, D.C.

Jack Hackett
Lieutenant
Senior Crime Scene Analyst
New York City Police Department
New York, New York

Randy Hanzlick, M.D.
Chief Medical Examiner
Fulton County Medical Examiner's Center
Associate Professor of Forensic Pathology
Emory University School of Medicine
Atlanta, Georgia

Rhea Haugseth, D.D.S.
Marietta, Georgia

Dale Heideman
Deputy Director

National Center for Forensic Science
University of Central Florida
Orlando, Florida

Roy Heim
Detective
Tulsa Police Department
Tulsa, Oklahoma

Edwin F. Huffine, Ph.D.
Director of Forensic Sciences Program
International Commission on Missing
  Persons
Sarajevo, Bosnia-Herzegovina

Louis Hupp
Supervisory Fingerprint Specialist
Federal Bureau of Investigation
Washington, D.C.

Robert A. Jensen
Vice President of Operations, Planning,
  and Training
Kenyon International Emergency
  Services, Inc.
Houston, Texas

Fred B. Jordan, M.D.
Chief Medical Examiner
State of Oklahoma
Oklahoma City, Oklahoma

Martin S. LaBrusciano
Chief (Retired)
Casselberry Police Department
Law Enforcement Consultant
Buffalo, Wyoming

Joel E. Lichtenstein, M.D.
Professor and Director, Gastrointestinal
  Radiology
Department of Radiology
University of Washington School of
  Medicine
Seattle, Washington

Mark Malcolm
Coroner
Pulaski County Coroner's Office
Little Rock, Arkansas

Acknowledgments

The National Institute of Justice (NIJ) thanks the members of the Technical Working Group for Mass Fatality Forensic Identification for their dedication to this project. NIJ also offers its gratitude to the agencies and organizations represented by the working group members.

In addition, NIJ thanks Carrie M. Whitcomb, Director; Jack Ballantyne, Associate Director, Biological Evidence; and John Bardakjy, Research Coordinator; of the National Center for Forensic Science for facilitating this project.

NIJ also thanks the law enforcement agencies, academic institutions, and commercial organizations worldwide that supplied contact information, reference materials, and editorial suggestions.

On February 18, 2003, the forensic community lost one of its leaders, Tom Shepardson, National Commander, Disaster Mortuary Operational Response Team (DMORT). Tom was a man of conviction, dedicated to his country, and a true believer that deceased individuals should be treated with the utmost respect and dignity. Tom believed that "we owe it to their families" to positively identify individuals and return them to their loved ones as quickly as possible. In essence, Tom Shepardson stood for everything this guide represents.

Contents

Section 1: Initial Response Considerations

Local agencies are advised to develop and implement an emergency management plan before a mass fatality incident. Federal assistance following a disaster may not be immediate and may not be forthcoming.

I. Determine the Scope of the Incident

Principle. A mass fatality incident can happen anywhere and usually without advance warning. When such an incident occurs, there are two phases to the response—

A. Stabilizing the scene and rescuing the injured.

B. Recovering and identifying human remains and evidence.

Procedure. It is important that responders en route to or arriving at the scene ask the following questions to comprehend the extent of the incident—

A. What happened?

B. Where did it happen?

C. How many injuries/fatalities are involved?

D. What are the known hazards?

E. What agencies are (or could become) involved?

F. Where is the scene command post located?

G. How will the scene be secured?

Summary. Answering these questions quickly will enable responders to notify and mobilize all appropriate resources. Keep in mind that the type and amount of resources needed may change as the investigation yields additional facts and details.

II. Know the Role of the Medical Examiner/Coroner

Principle. The medical examiner/coroner is responsible for establishing the cause and manner of death for the purposes of identifying the dead and issuing death certificates. Local/State statutes define the medical examiner/coroner's responsibilities.

Procedure. The medical examiner/coroner is responsible for overseeing and coordinating the provision and use of resources to recover and identify the dead. Initial considerations include—

A. Preparing morgue/autopsy facilities.

B. Establishing security and credentialing systems.

C. Coordinating the transportation of remains from the scene to the morgue.

D. Coordinating activities with the family assistance center (FAC), as appropriate.

E. Establishing communications and data management systems.

F. Establishing fiscal and material requirements.

G. Identifying the deceased.

H. Issuing death certificates.

I. Establishing a system for disposition of the remains.

Summary. The medical examiner/coroner's responsibilities include determining the cause and manner of death, identifying the dead, and returning the remains to the legal next of kin.

About the Authors

The Technical Working Group for Mass Fatality Forensic Identification is a multidisciplinary group of practitioners and subject matter experts from across the United States, Canada, and Eastern Europe. Each participant has experience with collecting, processing, and identifying human remains in the wake of a mass fatality incident.

III. Consider Additional Resources

Principle. The magnitude of a mass fatality incident may exceed the incident command's local capabilities and resources. If this happens, the incident command is expected to immediately begin contacting local, State, and Federal agencies for additional support (see appendix A for agency contact information).

These agencies are expected to assist with recovery/identification operations and provide administrative support. Depending on the nature of the incident, agencies (e.g., the National Transportation Safety Board [NTSB] and the Federal Bureau of Investigation [FBI]) are expected to respond immediately to the scene of the incident.

Procedure. The incident command should consider contacting the following local, State, and Federal resources if the scale of the incident exceeds available resources and capabilities—

A. Resources for the collection and identification of remains:

  1. Local and State resources:

    a. Medical examiner/coroner personnel.

    b. Law enforcement and fire departments.

    c. Canine search units.

  2. Federal/national resources:

    a. U.S. Department of Homeland Security, National Disaster Medical System:

      1) Disaster Mortuary Operational Response Teams (DMORT).

    b. Federal Bureau of Investigation (FBI):

      1) Critical Incident Response Group (CIRG).

      2) Evidence Response Team (ERT).

      3) Laboratory Services.

      4) Disaster Squad.

      5) Hazardous Materials Response Unit.

    c. U.S. Department of Justice, Office of Justice Programs:

      1) Office for Victims of Crime, Victim Assistance Center.

    d. U.S. Department of Defense (DoD):

      1) Armed Forces Institute of Pathology (AFIP):

        a) Office of the Armed Forces Medical Examiner (OAFME).

        b) Armed Forces DNA Identification Laboratory (AFDIL).

      2) U.S. Army Central Identification Laboratory, Hawaii (CILHI) [now Joint POW/MIA Accounting Command].

B. Additional resources:

  1. Local and State resources (in addition to the medical examiner/coroner):

    a. Crime laboratories.

    b. Emergency management offices.

    c. National Guard.

    d. State departments of transportation.

    e. Other.

  2. Federal/national resources:

    a. Federal Emergency Management Agency (FEMA):

      1) Urban Search and Rescue (US&R) Teams.

    b. National Transportation Safety Board (NTSB).

    c. Other.

3. Private resources:

   a. Nonprofit organizations.

   b. State funeral directors' associations.

   c. State dental associations and identification teams.

   d. Transportation companies.

   e. Private disaster response companies.

   f. Private forensic laboratories.

   g. Educational institutions.

Summary. Utilizing various resources can provide major assistance to local units of government.

Section 2: Arriving at the Scene

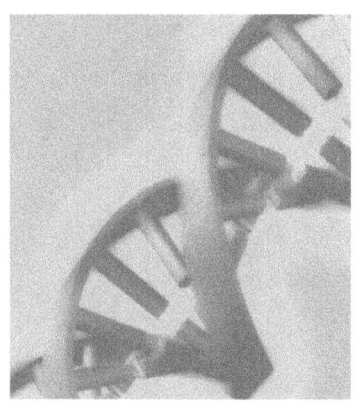

I. Initial Response and Evaluation

Principle. The initial response to a mass fatality incident establishes the incident management framework for the preservation of life and property and the thorough documentation and collection of all remains, personal effects, and evidence. The processing of evidence and human remains is secondary to emergency services and safety considerations. The recovery and collection process should be systematic and methodical to minimize the loss and contamination of evidence. First responders (i.e., the first public safety personnel to arrive at the scene, whether law enforcement officers, firefighters, or emergency medical services [EMS] personnel) should assess the scene quickly yet thoroughly to determine the course of action required. This assessment includes the scope of the incident, emergency services required, safety concerns, and evidentiary considerations.

Procedure. On arriving at the scene, first responders (e.g., fire, police, emergency medical personnel) are expected to—

A. Officially report to the incident command or highest ranking officer at the scene and produce appropriate credentials as required.

B. Maintain a written record, if possible, identifying all personnel and the time of their arrival on the scene.

C. Verify the type of incident (e.g., transportation, industrial, natural, or criminal) and request appropriate assistance.

D. Evaluate the scope of the incident:

1. Geographical extent (ensure the perimeter is large enough to encompass the entire scene).

2. Number of injuries/fatalities.

3. Identify eyewitnesses, if applicable.

E. Identify scene hazards such as structural collapse, chemical and biological hazards, and explosive devices.

F. Initiate appropriate EMS rescue procedures.

G. Leave the remains of the deceased undisturbed.

H. Establish an initial security perimeter to control entry to and exit from the scene.

I. Establish an incident command post and initiate an incident management system/incident command system (IMS/ICS) (see "Unified Incident Management System/Incident Command System" below for details).

J. Consider key personnel required to conduct the initial recovery and investigation operations.

Summary. Based on the preliminary evaluation of the scene, first responders are expected to identify scene hazards, request emergency services, and establish an incident command post.

II. Unified Incident Management System/Incident Command System

Principle. Initiating a unified IMS/ICS is essential for deploying and managing resources at the scene of a mass fatality incident. This system establishes a primary point of contact at the scene, an effective line of communication, and the authority to enforce scene safety and security. The incident command can use this system to coordinate search, rescue, and recovery efforts; establish staging areas; and allocate resources, including equipment, supplies, and personnel.

Procedure. The incident command is expected to implement the following procedures—

A. Establish the incident command center. Possible sites may include:

1. Airport hangar.

2. Auditorium.

3. Gymnasium.

4. Warehouse.

5. Tents and/or mobile units.

B. Evaluate the initial response to the incident and coordinate subsequent actions.

C. Establish staging area(s) for the assembly of the functional teams:

1. Police, fire, and EMS personnel.

2. Forensic recovery and identification specialists.

D. Establish other functional areas as required:

1. First aid center.

2. Temporary morgue. Possible sites may include:

    a. National Guard armory.

    b. Airport hangar.

    c. Warehouse.

3. Family assistance center (FAC). Possible sites may include:

    a. Hotel/motel.

    b. Conference/convention center.

    c. Auditorium.

4. Communication center.

5. Media staging area.

6. Briefing/debriefing area.

7. Stress management/support area.

E. Address other issues directly related to the recovery effort:

1. Parking areas.

2. Utilities/power supply.

3. Biohazard/refuse removal.

4. Storage areas for equipment and supplies.

5. Responder accommodations (including meals, lodging, and restrooms).

6. Administrative/operational resources:

    a. Office supplies/equipment.

    b. Electronic/computer equipment.

    c. Identification/recovery tools.

    d. Safety equipment.

    e. Vehicles.

Summary. The incident command is responsible for implementing a unified IMS/ICS to facilitate the coordination, documentation, and recovery/collection of remains, personal effects, and evidence. The incident command should use this system to secure the scene, manage and allocate resources, and ensure safety of all personnel involved in the rescue and recovery operations.

III. Scene Safety

Principle. Safety overrides all other concerns. First responders must take steps to identify and remove or mitigate safety hazards that may further threaten victims, bystanders, and public safety personnel. To avoid injuries to themselves and others, they must exercise due caution while performing emergency operations.

Procedure. Following the preliminary evaluation of the scene, first responders are expected to—

A. Assess and/or establish physical boundaries.

B. Request and/or conduct a safety sweep of the area by personnel qualified to identify and evaluate additional hazards and safety concerns.

C. Follow standard Environmental Protection Agency (EPA) and Occupational Safety and Health Administration (OSHA) regulations (see appendix A for agency contact information).

D. Follow standard precautions for potential nuclear, biological, and chemical hazards.

E. Mark hazard areas clearly and designate safety zones.

F. Communicate hazards to other personnel arriving at the scene.

G. Monitor the physical and psychological condition of personnel (e.g., dehydration, stress, and fatigue) and treat as necessary.

Summary. Safety is the overriding concern during emergency operations and the subsequent investigation. To ensure the safety of civilians and public safety personnel, first responders should take steps to identify, evaluate, and mitigate scene hazards and establish safety zones.

IV. Security and Control

Principle. First responders are responsible for establishing control and restricting scene access to authorized personnel.

Procedure. To establish scene security and control, first responders are expected to—

A. Set up a security perimeter.

B. Establish staffed entry/exit points.

C. Restrict access (e.g., by the media, bystanders, and nonessential personnel) into and out of the scene and secured areas through the security perimeter:

  1. Issue site-specific identification badges (for the FAC, temporary morgue, etc.), if possible.

  2. Maintain and update access logs/databases.

  3. Brief/debrief personnel when they enter or leave the staging areas.

D. Remove unauthorized personnel from the scene.

E. Establish staging areas:

  1. Parking area (for emergency response vehicles).

  2. Media staging area (for releasing information to the public about the incident).

Summary. First responders are expected to establish a controlled security perimeter and designate staging areas.

V. Rescue-to-Recovery Transition

Principle. The shift from search-and-rescue to search-and-recovery operations represents a major operating transition. The incident command is responsible for coordinating search-and-recovery efforts with the remains/evidence processing teams.

Procedure. The incident command, together with the remains/evidence processing team leaders, is expected to consider the following when shifting the operation from search and rescue to search and recovery—

A. Identify and select the remains/evidence processing team members.

B. Implement a simple, consistent, and expandable numbering system for remains, personal effects, and evidence.

C. Establish recovery and evidence processing procedures relevant to the type and extent of the incident.

> Regardless of the type of incident, consider all remains, personal effects, and other items recovered as evidence.

D. Document the location, collection, and removal of remains, personal effects, and other evidence.

E. Establish onscene staging areas to facilitate the efficient processing of collected items.

F. Assign rotating shift schedules.

G. Provide the remains/evidence processing teams with regular breaks, debriefings, and stress management.

Summary. The incident command is expected to implement procedures to initiate the transition between search-and-rescue and search-and-recovery operations.

Section 3: Processing the Scene

I. Initial Considerations

Principle. The complete and accurate identification of remains and evidentiary processing begins at the scene of the mass fatality incident. In most circumstances, the medical examiner/coroner has the ultimate responsibility for the recovery and identification of the deceased. The remains/evidence processing teams have to assume that any mass fatality scene could be a crime scene. They are expected to carefully document every piece of physical evidence recovered from the scene. The scene should be large enough to ensure its protection from public access until all agencies have agreed to release the scene. Although teams can discard information later, scene processing always involves the physical destruction of the actual scene, and additional information may not be recoverable after the scene has been processed and released. Efficient information recovery proceeds from the least intrusive to the more intrusive (e.g., taking photographs is allowed only after teams locate, flag, and sequentially number the remains). Although protocols may change in the middle of an event depending on the scope and extent of the incident, documenting every aspect of the remains/evidence processing operation will ensure the preservation of information.

Procedure. Before processing the scene, the incident command, in consultation with the medical examiner/coroner, is expected to—

A. Identify team leaders responsible for remains/evidence processing.

B. Determine the size and composition of the remains/evidence processing teams (usually a function of the team leaders), which may include:

1. Medical examiner/coroner.

2. Forensic anthropologist.

3. Odontologist.

4. Police crime scene investigator.

5. Forensic photographer.

6. Evidence technician.

7. Scribe/notetaker.

C. Integrate the remains/evidence processing teams according to existing interagency jurisdiction and chain of command. The scope and extent of the mass fatality incident determines the number of agencies involved.

D. Establish and/or verify control over access to the scene.

E. Establish communication among transport vehicles, the incident command, and the morgue.

F. Establish an onscene remains processing station.

G. Consider the recovery of remains and personal effects as evidence and preserve the chain of custody throughout the recovery operation.

Summary. Effective organization and composition of the remains/evidence processing teams ensures the proper collection and preservation of remains, personal effects, and evidence.

II. Establish a Chain of Custody

Principle. Establishing and maintaining a chain of custody verifies the integrity of the evidence. The remains/evidence processing teams are expected to maintain the chain of custody throughout the recovery process.

Procedure. Throughout the investigation, those responsible for preserving the chain of custody are expected to—

A. Document the time of arrival and departure of other personnel at the scene.

B. Establish a standard numbering system at the scene that relates back to the location of the remains/evidence.

> The remains/evidence processing teams are responsible for assigning numbers according to the order in which they locate and mark remains, personal effects, and evidence.

Ensure that the numbering system is:

1. Internally consistent and cross-referenced with other agencies.

2. Expandable.

3. Simple to interpret.

4. Capable of indicating where the remains, personal effects, and evidence were recovered.

5. Capable of tracking remains, personal effects, and evidence throughout the investigation.

6. Related to subsequent individual results without error.

7. Integrated into all protocols and reports.

C. Document the collection of evidence by recording its location at the scene and time of collection.

D. Document all transfers of custody (including the name of the recipient and the date and manner of transfer).

Summary. Maintaining the chain of custody by properly documenting, collecting, and preserving the evidence ensures its integrity throughout the investigation.

III. Scene Imaging and Mapping

Principle. The remains/evidence processing teams can use a grid system to divide the scene into manageable units to show the location and context of items (i.e., their positions relative to other items) at the scene. A grid system may need to be three-dimensional.

Procedure. The remains/evidence processing teams are expected to—

A. Record overall views of the scene (e.g., wide-angle, aerial, 360-degree) with a designated photographer to relate items spatially within the scene and relative to the surrounding area. A combination of still photography, videotaping, and other techniques is most effective. Remember to:

1. Consider muting the audio portion of any video recording unless there is narration.

2. Minimize the presence of scene personnel in photographs/videos.

3. Maintain photo and video logs.

B. Identify boundaries and fixed landmarks (e.g., a utility pole, building corners, or GPS-located points).

C. Establish a primary point of reference for the scene.

D. Divide the scene into identifiable sectors and create a checkerboard.

E. Use accurate measuring devices.

> **Suggestion:** Consider using steel tapes (which do not stretch) and electronic measuring/positioning devices. Consult with Department of Transportation officials, crime laboratory personnel, and local and State law enforcement agencies for models and specifications.

Summary. The remains/evidence processing teams are responsible for establishing an accurate, logical mapping system for the scene.

IV. Document the Location of Remains, Personal Effects, and Evidence

Principle. The remains/evidence processing teams are expected to include documentation in the permanent record of the scene. Photographic documentation creates a permanent record of the scene that supplements the written incident reports. The teams are expected to complete this documentation, including location information, before the removal or disturbance of any items. Videotaping may serve as an additional record but not as a replacement for still photography.

Procedure. The remains/evidence processing teams are expected to—

A. Photograph individual items (midrange and close) with an identifier (i.e., a grid identifier and/or individual item number) and scale. Consider including a directional compass arrow that points north.

B. Attach identifying numbers and flag all remains, personal effects, and evidence in the grid:

   1. Use a waterproof ink marker.

   2. Ensure that numbers on the flags correspond with those on the remains and are also clearly discernible in the photograph.

C. Ensure that the systematic onscene documentation of all remains, personal effects, and evidence includes:

   1. The sequential numbering system at the scene.

   2. Recovery location information.

3. Notes that may help with personal identification or scene reconstruction (e.g., generic descriptors, such as a foot or shoe).

4. Documentation of the evidence collector (e.g., the collector's unique identifier and the date and time of recovery).

D. Conduct the systematic removal of remains, personal effects, and evidence:

   1. Using a permanent marker, mark the outside of the primary bag or container and tag with the identifying number, the collector's unique identifier, and the date and time of collection.

   2. Place the same identifying number on the inside of the body bag or other bag or container.

   3. Do not remove any personal effects on or with the remains. Transport all personal effects on or with the remains to the morgue.

   4. When necessary, wrap the head before moving it to protect cranial/facial fragments and teeth.

> Do not assume that fragmented remains are associated with each other.

E. After removing the remains, photograph the areas from which evidence was recovered to document whether anything was under the remains.

F. After the remains/evidence processing teams have cleared the area and before releasing the scene for public access, conduct a final shoulder-to-shoulder sweep search to locate any additional items.

Summary. The remains/evidence processing teams must properly document the collection of all remains, personal effects, and evidence before removing them from the scene.

V. Onscene Staging Area

Principle. The remains/evidence processing teams should use the onscene staging area for checking documentation, maintaining the chain of custody, and conducting potential triage functions. At this area, the remains/evidence processing teams can add notes to aid personal identification at the morgue (e.g., comments about tattoos, marks, and scars) and identify contents of body bags (e.g., watches, body parts). The remains/evidence processing teams are responsible for closing and locking body bags at this point.

Procedure. The remains/evidence processing teams are expected to—

A. Establish a staging area proximate to the incident scene that provides maximum security from public and media scrutiny and access (including a no-fly zone over the site).

B. Remand evidence that is not required to accompany the remains to the mortuary to the custody of the appropriate agency.

C. Maintain the chain of custody of body bags:

    1. Maintain a log of the body bags that are transported from the staging area to the morgue.

    2. Record drivers' names and the license numbers of vehicles.

    3. Record dates and times that all vehicles leave for the morgue.

D. Maintain equipment and supplies at the staging area. Inventory resources may include:

    1. A large tent.

    2. Body/storage bags.

    3. Litters, gurneys, and stretchers for remains transport.

    4. Refrigeration vehicles.

    5. Emergency lighting.

    6. Sawhorses with plywood boards for makeshift examination tables.

    7. Tarpaulins or other screening materials to create visual barriers.

    8. Decontamination control.

    9. Inventory control system.

    10. Equipment storage.

    11. Personal protective equipment.

E. Notify the morgue when transport of remains will begin.

Summary. The remains/evidence processing teams are expected to maintain a secure triage area for initial examination of remains and other evidence and to ensure secure transport to the morgue. Strongly consider placing forensic identification specialists at the staging area, as initial evaluations at this point will dictate the efficiency of subsequent morgue operations.

Identification of Human Remains | **SECTION 4**

Section 4.1: Identification of Human Remains— Medical Examiner/Coroner

In addition to identification, the medical examiner/coroner should be aware of the role that bodies and fragments play in determining the cause and effect of the incident.

I. Define Expectations and Responsibilities

Principle. The medical examiner/coroner is responsible for the medicolegal investigation of the incident, including human factor considerations (e.g., toxicology). A mass fatality incident does not diminish this responsibility. The office of the medical examiner/coroner is in charge of the documentation, examination, identification, recovery, disposition, and certification of all remains as well as morgue operations. Additional assistance from other organizations and agencies is subject to the discretion and approval of the medical examiner/coroner.

If the medical examiner/coroner is not equipped to assume responsibility for managing morgue operations, a Disaster Mortuary Operational Response Team (DMORT) is responsible for appointing a forensic pathologist or temporary medical examiner/coroner who is capable of overseeing all morgue operations and administrative functions. The extent and role of a DMORT remains at the discretion of the local medical examiner/coroner.

Procedure. Following a mass fatality incident, the medical examiner/coroner is expected to—

A. Assume responsibility for the death investigation.

B. Review the scope of the incident.

C. Determine the need for additional assistance (e.g., Disaster Mortuary Operational Response Team [DMORT] and/or the Federal Bureau of Investigation [FBI] Disaster Squad) (see appendix B for details regarding DMORT activation).

D. Establish morgue operations and security.

E. Review and document the evidence.

F. Identify the deceased.

G. Appoint an individual responsible for organizing authorized site visits and for coordinating daily briefings/debriefings with the mass fatality task force, the victims' families, and the media.

H. Issue death certificates for all victims.

Summary. The medical examiner/coroner is expected to assume jurisdictional responsibility for conducting all aspects of the death investigation.

II. Establish Morgue Operations and Security

Principle. The medical examiner/coroner establishes morgue operations to ensure the proper collection, labeling, examination, preservation, and transportation of recovered remains. The medical examiner/coroner properly tags and inventories

each piece of evidence. This function also includes safeguarding all potential physical evidence and/or property and clothing that remain on the deceased.

Procedure. The medical examiner/coroner is expected to—

A. Limit access to entry/exit areas:

    1. Maintain and update a registry of solicited volunteers and their qualifications.

    2. Maintain and update a registry of unsolicited volunteers (whose services may or may not be required).

B. Issue/verify identification badges with photographs or other secure identifiers (e.g., thumbprints).

C. Determine/review staffing needs and ensure adequate facilities and equipment.

D. Differentiate normal from mass fatality morgue cases.

E. Assign reasonable work schedules.

F. Consider providing stress management counseling for the remains/evidence processing teams, morgue staff, and their families.

G. Maintain a daily activity log that records:

    1. The identification, reassociation, and disposition of all remains.

    2. An inventory of donated, loaned, or purchased items.

Summary. Implementing morgue operation and security procedures facilitates the proper identification of the deceased, maintains a proper chain of custody, and safeguards property and evidence.

III. Examine and Document Remains

Principle. The examination and documentation of remains provides detailed information about the deceased's physical attributes and the possible cause, manner, and circumstances of death. The medical examiner/coroner is responsible for maintaining all records and documentation, including notes, diagrams, photographs, radiographs/x-rays, fingerprints, and other images.

Procedure. The medical examiner/coroner is expected to—

A. Document where the remains were found and where death occurred.

B. Control and document how the remains are transported from the scene to the morgue.

C. Ensure that all remains are properly photographed.

D. Document the presence or absence of clothing and personal effects.

E. Diagram/describe in writing items of evidence and their relationship to the remains (with necessary measurements).

F. Document general physical characteristics.

G. Document the presence or absence of specific marks, scars, tattoos, and external prostheses:

    1. Ensure total body radiographs/x-rays are made (if indicated).

    2. Provide anthropological consultation (if indicated).

H. Document the presence or absence of injury/trauma.

I. Document fingerprints (and handprints, toe prints, or footprints if indicated).

J. Document the presence or absence of any items or objects that may be relevant (including internal prostheses, implants, etc.).

K. Document the dental examination (see "Section 4.6: Identification of Human Remains—Odontology" for procedures).

L. Collect appropriate DNA and toxicology samples (see "Section 4.4: Identification of Human Remains—DNA Analysis" for procedures).

M. Conduct a complete autopsy (if indicated).

Summary. The medical examiner/coroner evaluates and documents all evidence related to the remains to establish the identity of the deceased and determine the cause and manner of death.

IV. Collect, Inventory, and Secure Personal Effects and Evidence on/in Remains

Principle. Medical examiners/coroners are expected to safeguard the valuables and property of the deceased to ensure proper processing and eventual return to the legal next of kin. They also are expected to safeguard evidence on or near the remains to ensure its availability for further evaluation.

Procedure. The medical examiner/coroner is expected to ensure that all property and evidence is collected, inventoried, protected, and released as required by law according to the following functions—

A. Photograph the evidence (include an identification number with each photograph), including:

1. Remains.

2. Physical characteristics (e.g., tattoos, scars, or marks).

3. Wounds.

4. Personal effects (e.g., clothing and jewelry).

B. Collect associated physical evidence (e.g., explosives residue or other trace material).

C. Collect, inventory, and safeguard money at the scene and the morgue (with a witness present).

D. Collect, inventory, and safeguard personal valuables/property (e.g., clothing and jewelry) at the scene and the morgue:

1. Collect and store personal effects in paper bags (for airing and drying).

2. Clean each personal item removed from the remains (especially jewelry) and preserve with an appropriate identification number.

> Take DNA samples from personal effects before cleaning and cataloging them.

3. Use photographs when applicable for viewing and recognition by family members.

Summary. Collecting property and preserving evidence is critical for ensuring the chain of custody and admissibility in cases of legal action.

V. Establish Identification of the Deceased

Principle. Confirming the identity of the deceased is critical to the death investigation. Proper identification is necessary to notify the legal next of kin, resolve estate issues and criminal/civil litigation, and issue death certificates.

Procedure. The medical examiner/coroner is responsible for establishing the identity of the deceased using the following methods—

A. Presumptive:

   1. Direct visual or photographic identification of the deceased if visually recognizable.

   2. Personal effects (e.g., wallets, jewelry), circumstances, physical characteristics, tattoos, and anthropological data.

B. Confirmatory:

   1. Fingerprints (including handprints, toe prints, and footprints if indicated).

   2. Odontology.

   3. Radiology.

> The medical examiner/coroner is expected to conduct regular meetings with those assisting with the identification of the deceased to ensure concordance and resolve discrepancies before releasing the remains.

   4. DNA analysis.

   5. Forensic anthropology.

Summary. The medical examiner/coroner is expected to use all available methods of identification to confirm the identity of the deceased. Confirming identity is essential for resolving investigative, family, estate, judicial, and vital record issues.

Section 4.2: Identification of Human Remains— Administration/Morgue Operations

I. Establish Morgue Operations

Principle. Establishing morgue operations during a mass fatality incident may require expanded operations. The medical examiner/coroner is usually responsible for coordinating the logistical requirements to support sustained operations in an orderly environment.

Procedure. Consider the following functional areas in order to sustain the morgue operations from intake to release/disposition—

A. Identify the morgue operations supervisor, usually the medical examiner/coroner or designee, responsible for directly supervising the following individuals:

   1. Public information officer (PIO).

   2. Safety officer.

   3. Liaison officer for interagency coordination.

B. Identify the operations section leader (not necessarily a forensic specialist), who is expected to:

   1. Report directly to the medical examiner/coroner.

   2. Supervise the overall morgue operation.

C. Plan in advance of the incident for the use of forensic identification specialists (e.g., DNA analysts, fingerprint examiners, forensic anthropologists) who are expected to report to the medical examiner/coroner.

D. Establish the following resource management units:

   1. Resource unit (for tracking available resources and staff work schedules).

When the medical examiner/coroner requires teams of forensic specialists, ensure that team leaders are selected and introduced to the medical examiner/coroner. Team leaders are individuals designated to serve as the functional heads of forensic identification teams (e.g., fingerprints, forensic anthropology, odontology). They are responsible for organizing and directing the teams' activities. Effective team leaders typically have experience working a mass fatality incident and understand the forensic issues involved. Team leaders may also have specialized certifications in their disciplines.

   2. Situation unit (for collecting and entering data, preparing reports, and developing projections).

   3. Documentation unit (for organizing and maintaining all records).

   4. Demobilization unit (for releasing the scene).

Summary. Establishing an effective morgue operation helps ensure proper investigation, identification, and return of remains and personal effects to the legal next of kin.

II. Establish Workstation Flow

Principle. Ensuring the systematic and comprehensive examination of the remains effectively leads to a positive identification and preservation of evidence.

Procedure. The following functional activities are suggested in the order listed, but that order may be altered to accommodate the situation (see appendix C for workflow diagrams for forensic identification and forensic information management and coordination)—

A. Establish and secure an intake/admitting/triage area:

1. Assign escorts (one escort per body or set of remains).

2. Assign a case number.

3. Establish a case file.

4. Weigh (and measure if applicable) the remains.

5. Conduct triage.

B. Photograph remains and personal effects.

Summary. Effective and organized workstations at the morgue facility provide for an orderly and consistent operation and reduce the potential for error.

III. Establish a Forensic Identification Team

Principle. The medical examiner/coroner is responsible for establishing an identification team of specialists from a variety of forensic disciplines. These identification specialists are expected to compare antemortem to postmortem records and report their findings to the medical examiner/coroner for review and final approval.

Procedure. Depending on the extent of the incident, consider the following forensic identification specialists for comparing antemortem to postmortem records—

A. Evidence technician.

B. Fingerprint examiner.

C. Forensic anthropologist.

D. DNA analyst.

E. Odontologist.

F. Forensic photographer.

G. Pathologist.

H. Radiologist and radiographic technicians.

I. Toxicologist.

Summary. A forensic identification team is an essential part of the forensic investigation.

IV. Other Considerations

Principle. In addition to overseeing morgue operations, the medical examiner/coroner is expected to consider other details critical to the efficient collection, identification, documentation, and release of remains and personal effects.

Procedure. The medical examiner/coroner is expected to consider the following—

A. Use recognized, standard forms for the collection, collation, and matching of antemortem with postmortem records.

> Many of these sample forms are available through agencies via the Internet or on CD–ROM. Many of the agencies listed in appendix A offer electronic forms.

B. Establish and/or maintain a simple, concise, and continuous numbering system.

C. Conduct regular team briefings:

1. Consider scheduling and conducting daily briefings for all personnel involved.

2. Schedule briefings to cover shift changes, personnel transitions, duration of work, and rumor control.

D. Establish morgue security by restricting morgue access to authorized personnel.

E. Prohibit personal photography.

F. Monitor the physical condition and emotional well-being of those allowed to assist in the morgue operation.

Restricting access to the morgue preserves the integrity of the investigation, maintains the dignity of the deceased, limits exposure to chemical and biological hazards, minimizes the disruption of the chain of custody, restricts access to log documentation, and prevents the contamination of evidence.

G. Provide family support to members of the remains/evidence processing and morgue operation teams, including:

   1. Grief counseling.

   2. Phone/Internet access.

H. Recognize the contributions of first responders, morgue staff, and members of the various forensic identification teams after releasing the scene.

I. Maintain quality control.

Review records to ensure that all forms are accurate, legible, complete, and signed. Verify that all images are accounted for and logged.

Summary. Maintaining proper morgue operations helps to ensure a quality investigation that leads to the identification and disposition of the deceased.

Consider using the Internet and facsimile machines for the transfer of antemortem records and documents. Be aware that lines of communication may be down in the early hours following a mass fatality incident. Hard copies of documents must follow electronic transfer to ensure the chain of evidence.

Section 4.3: Identification of Human Remains—Forensic Anthropology

I. Role of the Forensic Anthropologist

Principle. The forensic anthropologist assists in the recovery and identification of remains following a mass fatality incident.

A forensic anthropologist has specialized training, education, and experience in the recovery, sorting, and analysis of human and nonhuman remains, especially those that are burned, commingled, and traumatically fragmented.

Procedure. In a mass fatality incident, the forensic anthropologist assists in the recovery, sorting, analysis, and identification of remains. Specifically, with regard to the identification of human remains, the forensic anthropologist is expected to—

A. Provide information concerning the biological characteristics (e.g., age at death, sex, race, and stature) of the deceased.

B. Assist the medical examiner/coroner in determining the circumstances surrounding the death of the individual.

Summary. The forensic anthropologist is expected to assist with the recovery, analysis, and identification of the remains.

II. Initial Evaluation

Principle. The specifics of the mass fatality incident determine the relative state of preservation and degree of fragmentation of the remains.

Procedure. The forensic anthropologist is expected to—

A. Evaluate and document the condition of the remains, including:

1. Complete remains.

2. Fragmented remains.

3. Burned remains.

4. Decomposed remains.

5. Commingled remains.

6. Any combination of the above.

B. Separate obviously commingled remains to calculate the minimum number of individuals, while ensuring continuity of the established numbering system.

C. Analyze the remains to determine sex, age at death, stature, and other distinguishing characteristics.

D. Assist in determining the need for additional analysis by other forensic identification disciplines (e.g., radiology, odontology).

E. Maintain a log of incomplete remains to facilitate future reassociation.

F. Document, remove, and save nonhuman and/or nonbiological materials for proper disposal.

Summary. The forensic anthropologist assesses the condition of the remains and assists in analyses.

III. Forensic Anthropological Analysis

Principle. The forensic anthropologist is expected to analyze the remains, depending on their condition, using various methods to determine biological attributes (e.g., age, sex, race, stature, and

idiosyncrasies). Even very small skeletal fragments may be useful in both personal identification and determination of the circumstances surrounding death.

Procedure. The forensic anthropologist is expected to evaluate, when possible, the following—

A. Sex.

B. Age at death.

C. Race.

D. Stature.

E. Antemortem pathological conditions (e.g., diseases or healed fractures).

F. Anomalies/abnormalities (including surgical hardware and prosthetic devices).

G. Perimortem trauma.

Summary. The forensic anthropologist is expected to use skeletal features to develop a biological profile.

IV. Additional Forensic Procedures

Principle. The forensic anthropologist is expected to assist in other procedures and use additional information from other forensic identification specialists in the analysis of remains.

Procedure. The forensic anthropologist is expected to assist with the following—

A. Obtaining DNA samples from soft tissue and bone.

B. Taking and interpreting radiographs/ x-rays.

C. Interpreting trauma (with the medical examiner/coroner).

D. Obtaining and isolating dental evidence.

E. Comparing antemortem and postmortem records.

Summary. The multidisciplinary approach to the identification process is vital to the successful response to and outcome of a mass fatality incident.

Section 4.4: Identification of Human Remains—DNA Analysis

I. Initial Considerations

Principle. For cases involving mass fatalities and/or highly fragmented remains, DNA provides an essential component of the identification process. DNA analysis can 1) identify the victims, 2) associate fragmented remains, and 3) assist in ongoing medical and legal investigations. The medical examiner/coroner is responsible for making the initial decision as to the primary goal of the DNA identification efforts: whether to pursue a medical legal finding of death for each victim or to identify all biological material recovered. This decision will have a significant impact on the scope of the identification process.

Procedure. The availability and utilization of DNA resources will vary according to the scope of the incident as well as the jurisdiction. The medical examiner/coroner is expected to evaluate the available DNA testing resources and establish formal agreements with laboratories capable of supporting the jurisdiction's mass fatality contingency plan.

A. *Resources.* The ready availability of high-throughput DNA analysis is capable of meeting the many complexities presented by larger mass fatality incidents and/or severe victim fragmentation. Smaller incidents may not require special resource considerations relating to specimen tracking and DNA analytical throughput. However, specimen tracking, data management, and the interpretation of results represent significant challenges. It is essential to have an inventory system available to log and track potentially tens of thousands of specimens. Testing laboratories are expected to use specialized software to facilitate the tracking, searching, and interpretation of large numbers of DNA profiles.

B. *Technology.* The medical examiner/coroner, in consultation with the DNA laboratory, is expected to determine which DNA analysis methods will be used to assist in the identification process.

C. *Timelines.* The medical examiner/coroner, in consultation with the DNA laboratory, is expected to establish realistic timelines for the completion of the DNA identification process based upon an assessment of the laboratories' capacities and data interpretation capabilities. The medical examiner/coroner is expected to resist adjusting timelines based on influences that could be detrimental to the overall identification effort.

Summary. Adequate resources and realistic timelines play a significant role in determining the extent to which DNA analysis may be used in the identification process.

II. Sample Collection for DNA Analysis

Principle. DNA analysis is a comparison science requiring one or more valid reference samples to identify human remains accurately. Three types of biological samples are collected to conduct DNA analysis—

A. Human remains.

B. Appropriate family references.

C. Direct references (e.g., biological specimens and personal effects).

Collect samples in a manner that prevents loss, contamination, or deleterious change and that involves the initiation of a proper chain of custody. Ensure that sample preparation includes provision for specimen

inventory, appropriate transport and storage of large numbers of samples, and accompanying documentation.

Procedure. Consider these following steps when collecting the following reference samples—

A. Human remains:

1. Collection:

    a. Collect, place, and appropriately store samples of suitable size in separately labeled containers (see appendix D for detailed DNA sample collection procedures).

    b. Store samples without preservatives (e.g., formaldehyde).

    c. When possible, collect samples from human remains for DNA analysis in conjunction with other forensic specialists at the designated morgue facility.

2. Documentation:

    a. Ensure that all remains submitted for DNA analysis have been photographed and documented at the designated morgue facility.

    b. Use a numbering system that is integrated or derived from the incident management system/ incident command system (IMS/ ICS) to uniquely identify each specimen. This can reduce transcription errors, minimize confusion, and reduce the possibility of misattribution that can arise from the use of alternative or redundant numbering systems. Avoid creating a new numbering system whenever possible.

3. Staff:

    a. Designate qualified staff members responsible for collecting samples for DNA analysis. This collection process may involve teams of two or more individuals:

        1) The staff member who takes the sample (e.g., the medical examiner/coroner or anthropologist) is expected to be able to assess its suitability for DNA analysis and identify the species and anatomical origin of the specimen.

        2) The staff member who records the sample verifies the sample description, assigns or maintains a unique identifier, maintains the chain of custody, and ensures proper storage (e.g., freezing the sample in a secure location).

    b. Request that the staff involved in collecting samples provide a DNA reference sample to be used for elimination purposes.

4. Samples for analysis. Take specimens for analysis from:

    a. Positively identified remains. Take samples for DNA analysis even if the remains have already been identified because the DNA results can be used for reassociation of fragmented remains, the identification of kindred victims, or elimination purposes.

    b. Fragmented remains. The medical examiner/coroner is expected to determine the goal of the identification effort and establish criteria for sample collection:

        1) Will all fragments be tested?

        2) Will only fragments meeting a certain size requirement be tested?

        3) Will only anatomically recognizable fragments be tested?

5. Preferred samples. Human remains sources include:

   a. Blood.

   b. Soft tissue:

      1) Deep red skeletal muscle.

      2) Organ tissue.

      3) Skin.

   c. Hard tissue:

      1) Bones.

      2) Teeth.

6. Sample handling:

   a. Tell staff members responsible for collecting DNA samples for analysis to take proper precautions to minimize the risk of contamination.

   b. Handle samples in a manner that prevents loss or deleterious change:

      1) Use sterile and disposable supplies for sample collection whenever possible.

      2) Discard or clean gloves and cutting instruments after taking each sample.

      3) Clean instruments, work surfaces, gloves, or other items with commercial bleach (one part bleach to nine parts water).

B. Family references:

   1. Collection:

     a. Initiate the collection of reference samples from members of the victims' immediate families at the family assistance center (FAC) or other designated sites.

     b. Develop and implement a plan to initiate the remote collection of reference samples from family members. Use other agencies to assist as necessary.

     c. Place and appropriately store individual reference samples in separately labeled containers.

   2. Documentation:

     a. Obtain and document informed consent using consent forms that have undergone legal review:

       1) Include the purpose for requesting the sample.

       2) Describe the intended use of the sample, restrictions on its use, and the confidentiality of the DNA results.

     b. Identify the donor:

       1) Confirm the donor's credentials.

       2) Clearly establish the donor's biological relationship to the victim.

       3) Obtain the donor's contact information.

       4) Use an appropriate form (see appendix E for DNA sample family reference collection forms).

     c. Originate and maintain a chain of custody for donor reference samples.

     d. Initiate a logical numbering system for all reference samples that is compatible with the IMS/ICS (e.g., consider allocating a predetermined block of numbers to assist in identifying the source of the sample).

   3. Staff:

     a. Identify and utilize appropriate individuals or agencies for the collection of family reference samples.

b. Train individuals to:

   1) Interact with victims' relatives with sensitivity.

   2) Use the proper collection methods (e.g., buccal swabs, fingerstick devices).

   3) Record accurate and reliable kinship information.

4. Preferred samples:

  a. Blood sample collected using venipuncture or a fingerstick device.

  b. Two properly collected buccal swabs.

5. Preferred donors. Collect the following types of samples from the preferred donors indicated:

  a. Short tandem repeat (STR) or other autosomal markers. Preferably, collect samples from the following:

   1) Either or both biological parents of the victim.

   2) The victim's mate and their biological children.

   3) Biological siblings who share the same parents as the victim.

  b. Mitochondrial DNA. Use maternally related family members as references.

  c. Y-chromosomal markers. Use paternally related family members as references.

> The suitability of the donor depends on the type of DNA analysis used. Consult the testing laboratories for clarification.

C. Direct reference samples:

1. Collection:

  a. Immediately establish a point of contact responsible for receiving and managing the collection of direct reference samples.

  b. Ensure that the FAC and other family services widely publicize the name or location of the point of contact and a list of items suitable for direct DNA referencing.

  c. Notify family members that they can submit direct reference samples at the same site where they provide family reference samples.

  d. Place and appropriately store individual reference samples in separately labeled containers.

2. Documentation:

  a. Obtain appropriate documentation to allow for the correlation of direct reference samples to a particular victim.

  b. Originate and maintain a chain of custody.

  c. Initiate a logical numbering system for all reference samples that is compatible with the IMS/ICS (e.g., consider allocating a predetermined block of numbers to assist in identifying the source of the sample).

3. Samples for analysis:

  a. Take care in choosing appropriate direct reference samples for analysis.

  b. Ensure that more than one item is submitted.

  c. Ensure that items are:

   1) Directly attributable to the victim.

   2) Submitted as soon as possible.

4. Preferred samples:

a. Biological samples suitable for testing include:

1) Bloodstain cards (e.g., Guthrie cards or cards obtained from other repositories).

2) Buccal swabs (e.g., home DNA identification kits).

3) Blood stored for elective surgery.

4) Pathology samples (e.g., biopsy samples, PAP smears).

5) Extracted teeth (e.g., baby or wisdom teeth).

6) Hair samples.

b. Personal items include:

1) Used toothbrushes.

2) Used shavers/razors.

3) Unwashed undergarments and other suitable clothing items.

4) Used personal hygiene items (e.g., feminine sanitary napkins).

5) Other personally handled or used items (consult the testing laboratory for specific criteria).

> Personal items may need to be returned to donors.

Summary. The proper selection, documentation, and handling of samples and corresponding reference submissions for DNA analysis can provide maximum assistance for identifying the deceased.

III. DNA Analysis Data Management

Principle. The process of accumulating, reviewing, and interpreting DNA data is the most challenging step when employing DNA technology to identify mass fatality victims. The difficulty of this task is compounded when more than one laboratory is involved in providing DNA results. Participating laboratories should affirm their mutual commitment, coordinate and track sample flow, and agree to use compatible software applications for data acquisition and interpretation.

Procedure. DNA data management requires a laboratory information management system (LIMS) to inventory, locate, maintain chain of custody, and document the disposition of samples—

A. Conduct DNA analysis at a single laboratory whenever possible to minimize complications associated with sample and data exchange.

B. Conduct DNA analysis at more than one testing facility if the scope of the incident exceeds a single laboratory's capabilities. In such an event, ensure that the participating laboratories support compatible software applications for sample tracking, testing data production, and subsequent interpretation:

1. Identify a single coordinating laboratory responsible for:

a. Evaluating methods.

b. Ensuring data quality.

c. Tracking sample flow between laboratories.

d. Ensuring data management.

e. Searching for matches between victim samples and appropriate reference samples.

f. Interpreting results.

g. Conducting administrative reviews.

2. Establish a secure, rapid means of data transmission between the laboratories.

3. Ensure that all laboratories use a sequential and consistent numbering system, including barcoding whenever possible.

C. Accumulate all data into a single database for interpretation.

Summary. Data management of the DNA analysis process can assist laboratories with the successful analysis of reference samples and the identification of the deceased.

IV. Outsourcing

Principle. In circumstances where the scope of the DNA analysis exceeds local capabilities, it may be necessary to subcontract DNA testing to one or more forensic DNA laboratories. Ensure that the capacities and capabilities of the selected laboratories are sufficient to meet the specific DNA analysis requirements.

Procedure. Consider the following when selecting subcontracted laboratories—

A. Employ specific guidelines to assess the abilities of laboratories before authorizing analysis. Criteria can include the following:

1. Accreditation by the American Society of Crime Laboratory Directors/Laboratory Accreditation Board (ASCLD/LAB) or certification by the National Forensic Science Technology Center (NFSTC) or other recognized accrediting/certifying organizations for compliance with national DNA standards.

2. Additional accreditation or certification as required to satisfy local jurisdictional criteria.

B. Confirm that laboratories have compatible DNA analysis methods, software applications, and modes of communication.

C. Confirm that laboratories have proven experience processing reference samples and remains from a mass fatality incident.

D. Assess the laboratories' capacities and competing priorities.

E. Maintain communication with participating laboratories throughout the identification process.

F. Evaluate the laboratories' performance through documentary review of previous audits or by conducting sample retesting, random reanalysis, and/or proficiency testing.

Summary. Strict selection criteria, appropriate quality review, and effective communication can help to ensure that the data generated by the subcontracted laboratories can be used with confidence for identification purposes.

V. Data Interpretation

Principle. DNA results can be analyzed and technically reviewed according to preestablished criteria. The interpretation of DNA analysis results within the context of the identification process can be conducted by the coordinating laboratory (or in-house laboratory, if one is available) before reporting the results to the medical examiner/coroner.

Procedure. The coordinating laboratory is expected to do the following before reporting DNA analysis results to the medical examiner/coroner—

A. Use appropriately validated DNA analysis protocols and review procedures.

B. Establish statistical criteria for kinship or direct reference matches, depending on the nature and scope of the incident.

C. Ensure the availability of appropriate software for storing and searching DNA profiles from victims and corresponding reference samples.

Some mass fatality incidents will require the capability to search large databases and clearly rank the significance of DNA matches. Consider making available individuals trained in the appropriate use of the computer software specifically used to develop kinship rankings.

D. Whenever possible, confirm DNA results from direct reference samples used for identification through kinship analysis or testing of a second direct reference sample.

E. Consider DNA identifications putative until they have undergone administrative review by the medical examiner/ coroner.

Summary. The proper interpretation and review of DNA analysis results will assist the medical examiner/coroner in the identification of victim remains.

Section 4.5: Identification of Human Remains—Fingerprints

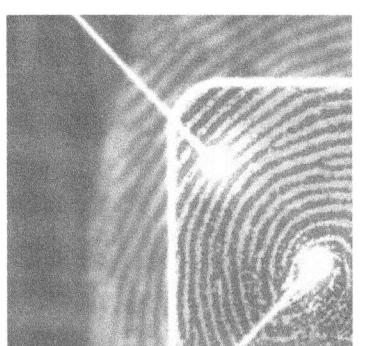

I. Initiate Preparation for Fingerprint Activities

Principle. Fingerprint identification is a positive means of identifying unknown victims and confirming the identification of those who are tentatively identified by other means (e.g., witness descriptions or photographs).

Procedure. When it appears that the identification of mass fatality incident victims may be made or expedited by fingerprint identification, implement the following procedures—

A. Obtain a list (e.g., a passengers' manifest or employment records) and description (e.g., sex and date of birth) of possible victims:

   1. Obtain antemortem prints and document their source.

   2. Establish a log of antemortem prints.

   3. Establish antemortem and postmortem print files.

B. Establish onscene protocols for the protection of fingerprints, palm prints, and footprints during collection and recovery operations. The protection of the hands, fingers, and feet by the remains/evidence processing teams is of paramount importance.

C. Establish document control and maintain the chain of custody.

D. Consult with the medical examiner/coroner and other forensic identification specialists to establish morgue protocols before processing the remains.

Summary. Appropriate preparation and documentation is essential for the successful identification of individuals by fingerprint examination.

II. Prepare Morgue for Postmortem Fingerprint Examination

Principle. The fingerprint processing of remains, especially those that have been burned or have sustained appendage trauma, may be a long and tedious function involving the use of surgical instruments, chemicals, and fingerprinting equipment.

Procedure. A fingerprint processing area can include—

A. Waist-high gurneys.

B. Comparison work area.

C. Specialized equipment (usually provided by the fingerprint examiner).

D. Desk lighting and running water.

E. Appropriate airtight containers to store fingers, toes, and any ridge material.

Summary. Fingerprinting remains may be a long and difficult process. The morgue facility is expected to provide a properly equipped, safe, and adequate workspace to facilitate the identification process.

III. Commence Print Processing

Principle. In conjunction with the medical examiner/coroner, the fingerprint examiner is responsible for processing remains in an effort to record friction ridge skin for the purpose of identification.

Procedure. When processing remains for fingerprints, palm prints, and footprints, the fingerprint examiner is expected to—

A. Initiate and maintain an examination/activity log.

B. Record and verify available identifying data (e.g., body number, basic descriptors).

C. Photograph remains/friction ridge surfaces before processing.

D. Examine for and collect trace evidence from friction ridge surfaces.

E. Prepare friction ridge skin for printing.

F. Obtain authorization from the medical examiner/coroner before removing fingers or hands:

  1. Label all removed body parts immediately.

  2. Ensure that all labeled body parts are reassociated with the appropriate body.

G. Print all available friction ridge skin on hands and feet.

H. Document the fingerprint examination process:

  1. Record the name of the fingerprint examiner (printed and signed) and date of examination on the fingerprint card.

  2. Document and log the number(s) assigned to the body/remains (including designation and descriptors) on the fingerprint card.

  3. Document friction skin area recorded as well as areas not available or unsuitable for recording.

> It may become necessary to fingerprint survivors of the incident for exclusionary purposes.

Summary. When processing remains for identification, the fingerprint examiner is expected to record friction ridge surfaces printed, document the processes employed, and maintain legible and accurate records.

IV. Conduct Comparison and Identification

Principle. The comparison of antemortem fingerprint records with those obtained directly from the remains by the fingerprint examiner may lead to the positive identification of the deceased.

Procedure. Upon obtaining the antemortem fingerprint records of potential mass fatality incident victims, the fingerprint examiner is expected to—

A. Compare antemortem with postmortem prints.

B. Identify a second qualified fingerprint examiner to verify all identifications (consistent with discipline standards) and document the findings on the postmortem card.

C. Initiate automated fingerprint identification system (AFIS) searches in available databases if no antemortem prints are present.

D. Notify the medical examiner/coroner of each identification in a timely manner.

E. Comply with jurisdictional protocol for the retention or disposition of documents.

Potential sources of known fingerprints include employment and government/military service records. In some cases, latent handprints and footprints can be obtained by qualified personnel from homes, businesses, or personal effects of suspected victims.

Summary. Friction ridge skin provides a proven means of identification. Only qualified fingerprint examiners are expected to make and certify comparisons and identifications.

Section 4.6: Identification of Human Remains— Odontology

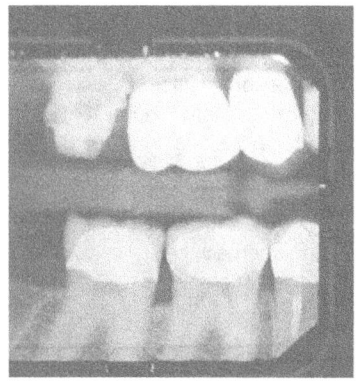

I. Preparation

Principle. Dental identification is a scientific and legally accepted form of human identification. The creation of the forensic dental team before a mass fatality incident is critical to a successful operation at the incident scene. The dental team leader is ultimately responsible for the entire dental team. The dental team leader is also responsible for coordinating activities with other agencies (e.g., Disaster Mortuary Operational Response Team [DMORT], Federal Bureau of Investigation [FBI], National Transportation Safety Board [NTSB]) and forensic identification disciplines (e.g., forensic anthropology, fingerprints, radiology).

Procedure. The designated dental team leader is expected to—

A. Establish a forensic dental identification team that includes antemortem, postmortem/radiology, and comparison/computer teams.

B. Create a dental organizational chart to ensure the proper scheduling and management of the dental team.

C. Establish sources of antemortem information and liaison with the family assistance center (FAC) (through the NTSB or another designated organization/agency) if available.

D. Assign a team member to work with other forensic identification specialists and update the missing persons master list.

E. Select the proper (printed and electronic) forms:

1. Use standard forms for the entire operation (see appendix A for links to the forms listed below):

a. Domestic forms (e.g., WinID or Victim Identification Program [VIP]).

b. International forms (e.g., Disaster Victim Information [DVI]).

2. Consider computer software for storing and comparing records and radiographs/x-rays (Digital Imaging and Communications in Medicine [DICOM]-compliant if possible).

F. Determine required equipment/ supplies:

1. Establish arrangements with suppliers. Mobile equipment can greatly increase the flexibility of the dental team.

> Consider the Disaster Mortuary Operational Response Team (DMORT) as a source for equipment, supplies, and personnel following a mass fatality incident (see appendix B for information about DMORT activation).

2. Inventory the material assets that are available onscene to the dental team.

Summary. Preparation and training before an actual mass fatality incident are recommended. Proper preparation can facilitate the smooth and effective operation of the dental team.

II. Collect and Preserve Dental Evidence

Principle. In a mass fatality incident, bodies may be fragmented. Forensic odontologists are valuable at the scene to assist in the recognition, documentation, and preservation during transport of dental

remains. A variety of antemortem dental references may assist in the identification process.

Procedure. The dental team is expected to—

A. Identify, collect, and preserve dental evidence:

1. Consider wrapping the craniofacial remains (i.e., the head) at the scene to prevent loss of teeth.

2. Examine the body bag for possible loose dental remains and consider the use of large format (whole body/screening) radiography.

3. Consider onscene dental radiographs/x-rays for fragile evidence that may not survive transport to the morgue.

B. Assist other forensic identification specialists (e.g., anthropologists and pathologists) with recognizing dental evidence.

C. Request original antemortem dental information (including radiographs/x-rays, films, photographs, casts, and electronic images) through the FAC or another designated agency/organization if available.

> The family assistance center (FAC) can expedite the authorization of records to facilitate communication between the dental team and the victims' dentists.

Summary. Dental remains, which might be fragile and difficult to identify, may provide the only evidence for securing a positive identification of the victim. The dental team is expected to assist other forensic identification specialists as necessary.

III. Dental Records

Principle. Dental identification requires the comparison of antemortem with postmortem dental findings. These two types of dental records will reflect the comprehensive antemortem dental information (collected on a single form or record if possible) with the dental autopsy results. When questions arise, engage in dentist-to-dentist discussions.

Procedure. The following approach can ensure the proper documentation of dental identification procedures—

A. Antemortem dental examination:

1. Establish a contact/liaison with the agency or organization responsible for collecting antemortem dental information (e.g., the FAC, FBI, sheriff, or medical examiner/coroner's office).

2. Consolidate individual antemortem dental information (e.g., medical and dental records, photographs, and radiographs/x-rays) into a single, comprehensive antemortem dental form/record using a standard charting format. This is perhaps the most important part of the dental identification operation.

> Be aware of different dental numbering systems (e.g., left versus right) and radiograph/x-ray mounting techniques (see tables for dental numbering systems in appendix F).

3. Consider using computer-assisted programs to assist with the sorting and storage of both antemortem and postmortem information.

4. Review relevant local, State, and Federal statutes to determine how to obtain antemortem information.

> The dental team leader can ensure quality control over the dental identification process by 1) assigning two or more individuals to each dental team and 2) reviewing (or assigning a designee to review) and approving all forms/records before the release of remains.

B. Postmortem dental examination:

1. Perform extra/intra-oral photography (either conventional or digital) as required.

2. Obtain radiographs/x-rays:

   a. Obtain postmortem radiographs/x-rays (either conventional or digital) according to guidelines recommended by the American Board of Forensic Odontology (ABFO).

   b. Ensure that the postmortem dental team leader reviews all postmortem radiographs/x-rays for quality control.

> Perform facial dissection to gain access only if required and approved by the medical examiner/coroner for clinical and radiographic examinations. If resection (i.e., removing the jaw fragment) is required, then it is imperative to label and bag these specimens and ensure they remain with the body.

3. Conduct the clinical examination:

   a. Conduct a clinical examination to document postmortem dental findings.

b. Assign more than one dental team member to conduct the examination and review results for quality control.

4. Consolidate postmortem dental information (e.g., medical and dental records, photographs, and radiographs/x-rays) onto a single, comprehensive postmortem dental record/form using a standard charting format.

Summary. The dental team can accomplish dental identification if there is adequate documentation of antemortem and postmortem evidence (e.g., clinical charting of dental procedures, radiographs/x-rays, and photographic documentation of dental restorations, skeletal landmarks, or disease conditions).

IV. Compare Records

Principle. Dental identification is possible by comparing identified antemortem documentation with postmortem documentation of unknown remains from the incident scene.

Procedure. The dental team is expected to—

A. Compare summarized antemortem and postmortem information.

> Two methods can be used for comparing antemortem with postmortem information: 1) comparing hard copies manually by walking around a series of tables/view boxes or 2) using computer-assisted programs to prioritize a list of possible matches.

B. Ensure the mandatory peer review of the antemortem, postmortem, and comparison record processes.

C. Establish procedures for contacting dentists of record if the dental team requires additional dental information.

Summary. Dental identification requires the comparison of antemortem and postmortem information. Dental identification teams involved in comparing information are expected to consider all methods available, including clinical restoration, skeletal (i.e., jaw and skull) anatomy, and observable diseases. Compare records according to standardized protocol. The dental team leader is expected to ensure the complete documentation of this comparison process.

V. Final Comparison and Identification

Principle. The dental team can make a dental identification by comparing a known reference (i.e., antemortem information) with dental information from unidentified remains. This process contributes to the final report issued by the medical examiner/coroner.

Procedure. The dental team is expected to—

A. Use a comparison/summary form (i.e., one that incorporates text and/or graphical comparison data [e.g., WinID odontogram or radiographs/x-rays]) of the dental/anatomic similarities for both antemortem and postmortem dental information.

B. Arrive at a conclusion (after comparing antemortem with postmortem dental information) reflected in the four categories below:

1. Positive dental identification.

2. Possible (i.e., "consistent with") dental identification.

> The term "consistent with" implies a possible identification. Although it does not connote a positive identification, it helps prioritize a possible identification by other means.

3. Exclusion.

4. Inadequate information for comparison.

C. Submit the signed and verified comparison document (e.g., a letter, a form, or an image-enabled report featuring pictures of radiographs/x-rays) to the medical examiner/coroner.

Summary. The primary mission of the dental team is generating identification conclusions and reporting them to the medical examiner/coroner.

Section 4.7: Identification of Human Remains—Radiology

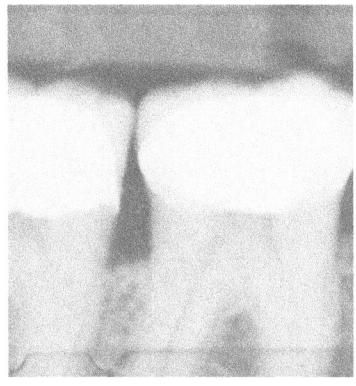

I. Introduction

Radiology provides vital support to the medical examiner/coroner. The radiologist conducts radiograph/x-ray examinations to detect radiopaque evidence; identifies remains by comparing antemortem with postmortem radiographs/x-rays; and assists pathologists, anthropologists, and odontologists in the interpretation of radiographs/x-rays. The medical examiner/coroner should consider establishing a radiology team early on in the investigation process.

II. Equipment/Supplies

Principle. The radiology team should use the necessary equipment and supplies to radiograph/x-ray remains.

Procedure. The radiology team leader is expected to—

A. Address radiation safety issues such as shielding.

B. Identify sources of equipment or additional facilities.

III. Radiographs

Principle. Take radiographs/x-rays of all recovered remains before forensic processing. The radiology team may use additional imaging for clarification of details and potentially for primary radiographic identification. The radiology team leader is expected to check all radiographs/x-rays for supporting or exclusionary information before the release of the remains.

Procedure. The radiology team is expected to—

A. Conduct an initial radiograph/x-ray of the remains.

B. Conduct additional radiographs/x-rays as requested by other forensic specialists.

C. Appreciate special considerations (e.g., making radiographs/x-rays of the hands and feet of the flight crew) as they relate to the incident.

D. Assist with the comparison of antemortem and postmortem radiographs.

Summary. Radiology is a vital early step in processing the remains, supporting or excluding potential identification and potentially serving as a primary means of identification.

Section 4.8: Identification of Human Remains— Antemortem Data Collection

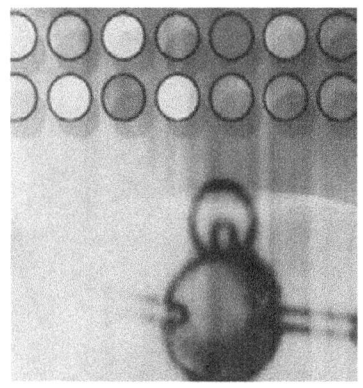

Principle. The medical examiner/coroner may identify the deceased by the prompt and efficient use of samples and data from families, individuals, and public and private organizations. The data may be in electronic and/or printed form. The medical examiner/coroner must have unrestricted, rapid access to antemortem medical, dental, and other records for comparison.

The Aviation Disaster Family Assistance Act of 1996 establishes procedures for contacting the legal next of kin to request antemortem data. Federal law restricts the degree to which airline personnel are involved in the collection of antemortem data and samples. In non-transportation-related incidents, a local or State government representative may assume these responsibilities.

Procedure. The following are some but not all of the factors that the appropriate administrator is expected to consider in establishing a family assistance center (FAC)—

The type of mass fatality incident determines who is responsible for establishing and opening the family assistance center (FAC):

■ In the event of an aviation disaster, the air carrier is expected to establish and staff the FAC.

■ In the event of a natural disaster, the medical examiner/coroner is expected to consult local, State, and nongovernmental assistance agencies.

■ For other types of disasters, consult with the primary industry involved.

A. Before the legal next of kin arrive, identify a location and establish a site where they can meet to provide antemortem data and sample records (e.g., a hotel, auditorium, or conference center).

B. Consider the following recommendations as a checklist for the FAC:

1. Be prepared to meet the families as they arrive.

2. Assist when necessary in coordinating activities to meet the families' physical and mental needs.

3. Control who gains access to the FAC.

4. Conduct briefings with the families as necessary.

5. Provide a liaison between the families and the agencies involved when needed.

6. Be prepared to collect antemortem data and provide it to the appropriate agencies as required:

   a. Ensure that interview rooms are private and quiet.

   b. Schedule and document all interviews with the legal next of kin.

   c. Limit the number of legal next of kin in each interview room.

   d. Require all interviewed legal next of kin to complete a personal interview form.

7. Maintain confidentiality and the trust of the families.

8. Consider any additional processes that the incident may require. Flexibility is the key word in this process.

C. Contact the legal next of kin not present at the FAC:

1. Schedule appointment times to contact family members.

2. Review antemortem collection procedures with family members over the telephone.

3. Ensure that the interview is private and confidential.

4. Complete a personal interview form following each telephone interview.

D. Identify antemortem data/sample resources:

1. Samples provided by the legal next of kin:

   a. Dental records.

   b. Medical records (including antemortem radiographs/x-rays).

   c. Fingerprints (derived from law enforcement, military, and employment records).

   d. Photographs.

   e. Biological samples (e.g., tissue blocks, slides, and DNA reference samples).

> The medical examiner/coroner or designee may need to have victim records in foreign languages translated. See "Section 6: Other Issues" for details.

E. Establish a location to receive all incoming antemortem data and samples (expected to be sent via an express delivery service or brought to a receiving area other than the morgue by a family member).

F. Notify the legal next of kin when antemortem data and samples have been received.

G. Maintain a log of all incoming data/samples.

H. Direct all data/samples to the morgue for review and analysis.

Summary. Consider the wide range of antemortem information that can aid in identification.

Section 5: Disposition of Human Remains, Personal Effects, and Records

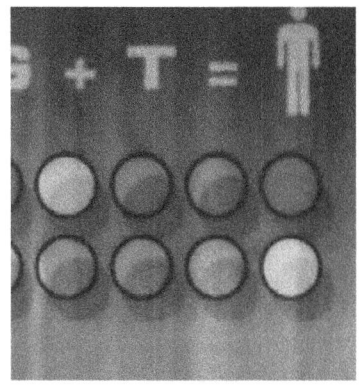

I. Issuing the Death Certificate

Principle. The documentation of the identification, cause, manner of death, and final disposition are required by law and used for vital statistics and the initiation of probate.

Procedure. Medical examiners/coroners are expected to complete their portion and transmit the document with the release of the remains. As part of this process, they are expected to—

A. Issue the death certificate.

B. Record when appropriate the death certificate in the county or territory where the remains were recovered.

> Review local and State laws to determine the office/agency responsible for filing death certificates (usually the office of vital statistics).

C. Issue a court-ordered certification of death when no human remains are recovered or scientific efforts for identification prove insufficient.

Summary. The death certificate is the legal document that states the identification, cause and manner of death, demographic information, and final disposition of the remains.

II. Disposition of Remains

Principle. Every family is expected to have the opportunity to involve itself in the decisionmaking process for the disposition of remains. Public health issues associated with a mass fatality incident, however, may dictate the manner of disposition of the remains.

Procedure. The medical examiner/coroner is expected to follow rules regarding the notification of the legal next of kin. Where appropriate, in cases of fragmentation and commingling, the medical examiner/coroner is expected to explain to the families the options for disposition of any subsequently identified remains before releasing incomplete remains (see appendix G for a sample authorization form to release remains).

A. Facilitate coordination between the family assistance center (FAC) or designated agency and local medicolegal authorities:

1. Notify the legal next of kin after establishing identification according to State and territorial laws.

2. If necessary, obtain additional instructions regarding the disposition of remains.

B. Release all identified body parts submitted for special studies related to the identification process (except those specimens consumed by analysis or retained for further study).

Summary. This process can facilitate the timely and dignified return of the remains, allowing the families to grieve, memorialize their loved ones, settle estates, and resolve legal issues.

> Different methods exist for the disposition of unidentified or unclaimed remains. If the remains are unidentified or identified but unclaimed, consider disposition according to local custom or statute. The medical examiner/coroner can consider accessing the unidentified remains later as a desirable option.

III. Return of Personal Effects

Principle. Mass fatality incidents produce items physically on the human remains (associated) and items not directly on but adjacent or within close proximity to the human remains (unassociated). Associated items accompany the remains to the morgue. The medical examiner/coroner is expected to document these items, apply them toward the identification process if required, and facilitate their return. The medical examiner/coroner also is expected to implement a mechanism to safeguard cash and valuables.

Procedure. The medical examiner/coroner is expected to accomplish and document the following to ensure the chain of custody—

A. Release associated/unassociated personal effects to the agency designated to receive those effects:

   1. Follow existing local protocol governing the release of personal effects if no such agency exists.

   2. Consider legislation such as the Aviation Disaster Family Assistance Act of 1996, where applicable.

B. Release unclaimed personal effects to the agency designated to receive those effects or dispose of them according to existing local protocol.

Summary. Treat all recovered personal effects with care because of their importance in the identification process as well as their intrinsic value to the families.

IV. Special Considerations

Principle. Mass fatalities produce unique challenges that the medical examiner/coroner should address when coordinating the disposition of remains and personal effects.

Procedure. The medical examiner/coroner is expected to consider the following potential issues and consult with appropriate specialists as required—

> The medical examiner/coroner is expected to conduct regular meetings with those assisting with the identification of the deceased to ensure concordance and resolve any discrepancies before the remains are released.

A. Review the work of each forensic identification team before releasing remains to the legal next of kin.

B. Validate and consolidate all missing persons lists (e.g., flight manifests, hotel registries, and employee lists).

C. Understand the legal issues (e.g., international law and treaties, maritime laws, health regulations, and hazardous materials [HAZMAT] protocols).

D. Respect religious and cultural considerations.

E. Identify the legal next of kin according to State and territorial law.

Summary. Legal, cultural, and operational concerns require evaluation of each mass fatality incident from many different perspectives.

V. Archiving Records

Principle. The medical examiner/coroner is expected to keep all records and supporting documents pertaining to the recovery, identification, and disposition of remains and personal effects for future reference as required by statute.

Procedure. The medical examiner/coroner can ensure the appropriate storage, security, preservation, and retrieval of records and supporting documents by—

A. Archiving and cross-referencing records that can be retrieved as individual or group files for quick reference at any time.

B. Using electronic storage and retrieval methods, if available, to archive records.

Summary. Properly archived records allow for prompt retrieval of detailed information when requested for legal, information, or research purposes.

A case involving an ongoing criminal investigation is exempt from release under State public records laws. Medical, dental, psychiatric, and prescription histories do not lose their privacy status and are not subject to the public records laws even after they are placed in the medical examiner/coroner's case file.

Section 6: Other Issues

I. Reimbursing Local and State Agencies

Principle. Mass fatality response operations incur expenses related to staffing, supplies, and equipment. Local/State emergency management departments should have the appropriate documents and procedures in place before a mass fatality incident occurs within their jurisdiction.

Procedure. The appropriate administrator is expected to—

A. Understand the regulations regarding reimbursement issues.

B. Provide a responsible fiscal representative to oversee the creation of financial and expense records.

C. Provide supporting documents to verify:

   1. The number and types of personnel involved.

   2. The number of hours worked by each individual.

   3. The agencies involved.

   4. The supplies and equipment used.

   5. The services contracted.

D. Coordinate with other responsible agencies.

E. Understand that some costs may be long term, including:

   1. Legal considerations.

   2. Employee health/mental health followup issues.

   3. Disposition of evidence, remains, and records.

Summary. Reimbursement for personnel, supplies, equipment, and other related

> In aviation incidents, the air carrier may be responsible for some expenses incurred in the recovery and identification of remains.

expenses is a critical consideration that requires careful planning and thorough documentation.

II. Implementing a Transition Plan

Principle. Effective operations require continuity of services.

Procedure. The appropriate administrator is expected to—

A. Establish criteria for daily shift changes.

B. Establish criteria for the implementation of replacement teams.

C. Facilitate the communication of information between teams.

D. Plan regular meetings between incoming and outgoing teams.

E. Hold regularly scheduled functional specialty meetings.

Summary. Effective planning and communication through regularly scheduled meetings can foster the exchange of information between the agencies and individuals involved in the investigation.

III. Mutual Assistance Agreements

Principle. Mutual aid statutes and memoranda of understanding (MOUs) provide for assistance from other jurisdictions in obtaining required support services and equipment.

Procedure. The appropriate administrator is expected to—

A. Understand that jurisdictional and liability issues may affect the implementation of mutual assistance agreements.

B. Understand the scope of services available through existing mutual aid statutes and how to implement such services.

C. Identify additional needs for support and invoke additional MOUs specifying when and how these services may be implemented.

D. Know that the National Association of Counties (NACO) and similar organizations maintain information and model plans on mutual aid (see appendix A for agency contact information).

Summary. Prior planning and implementation of mutual assistance agreements and MOUs are critical to ensure cooperation and coordination in the provision of available services.

IV. Release and Control of Information

Principle. Information regarding the recovery and identification operations is a critical element that affects the family members and the overall operation. As a result, information released to the media and the public must be managed appropriately.

Procedure. The appropriate administrator is expected to—

A. Initiate and enforce uniform procedures determining the release and management of information. Recovery and identification personnel should refrain from unauthorized communication with the media.

> Be aware that families of the deceased require special consideration in the release and management of information. Early, regular contact with families to provide information is critical.

B. Designate a public information officer (PIO) to coordinate the release of information. Direct all media inquiries to the PIO.

C. Establish categories of information for release to the media, families, agencies, and other parties.

D. Use caution when discussing specific disaster-related issues away from the scene.

E. Brief all personnel on a regular basis regarding the sensitivity of information.

Summary. Proper management and release of information are necessary considerations to protect the integrity of the response.

V. Scene Demobilization (Postincident Activities)

Principle. The demobilization of agencies and individuals assigned to process a mass fatality scene requires careful planning. The participating agencies are expected to implement scene demobilization procedures only after the scene is ready for release.

Procedure. The appropriate administrator is expected to—

A. Establish a demobilization plan that includes the following:

1. Ensure appropriate decontamination of equipment and facilities.

2. Return donated/loaned equipment and supplies.

3. Conduct postincident debriefings.

4. Consult regularly with the other agencies involved.

5. Recognize the efforts of the agencies and individuals who responded to the incident and processed the scene.

B. Reduce staff in a coordinated fashion based on circumstances and the duration of the investigation.

C. Prepare a formal after-action report citing optimal practices and lessons learned.

Summary. Planning from the beginning for the demobilization of the response effort can facilitate the smooth transition of jurisdictional authority.

VI. Stress Management

Principle. Stress can negatively affect the responders, their coworkers, and the overall efficiency of incident operation. The response to a mass facility incident should include systems to deal with stress, whether psychological, physiological, acute, or long term.

Procedure. The appropriate administrator is expected to—

A. Establish a plan for recognizing and managing stress using personnel trained in mass fatality stress management.

B. Consider briefing response personnel on stress issues before their assignment.

C. Provide peer and professional support to observe and treat personnel who may be experiencing stress.

D. Organize the response to prevent stress and accommodate individual behavior.

E. Plan postincident stress debriefings for responders and volunteers.

Summary. The psychological impact on mass fatality responders is real and needs to be addressed before, during, and after the incident.

VII. Volunteers

Principle. Volunteers may appear at the scene of a mass fatality incident regardless of the need for their services. Carefully consider choosing and using volunteers. Volunteers are expected to be used according to their knowledge, skills, and abilities as well as within liability limitations.

Procedure. The appropriate administrator is expected to—

A. Determine the need for volunteers.

B. Maintain a roster of volunteers' names with updated contact information.

C. Establish criteria for verifying the credentials and qualifications of volunteers. Be wary of volunteers with ulterior motives.

D. Develop a procedure to match volunteers with operational needs according to their knowledge, skills, and abilities.

E. Ensure that volunteers are supervised by an appropriate official.

Summary. Although volunteers may be helpful in some situations, cautiously review their credentials and qualifications for the duties and functions required.

VIII. Language, Cultural, and Religious Considerations

Principle. Language and cultural differences may complicate all parts of the mass fatality response and should be considered in the overall plan.

Procedure. The appropriate administrator is expected to—

A. Identify language service resources beforehand (e.g., colleges and universities, embassies, hospitals, and the U.S. Department of State). These resources may be valuable in interpreting antemortem information regarding foreign victims.

B. Respect the cultural and religious differences that exist in response to death.

C. Consider using local/regional religious officials when addressing these differences.

Summary. Give advance consideration to language, cultural, and religious differences when planning the response.

Appendix A. Resources and Links

American Academy of Forensic
 Sciences (AAFS)
P.O. Box 669
Colorado Springs, CO 80901–0669
719–636–1100
http://www.aafs.org

American Board of Forensic Anthropology
 (ABFA)
http://www.csuchico.edu/anth/ABFA

American Board of Forensic Odontology
 (ABFO)
http://www.abfo.org

American Red Cross
http://www.redcross.org

American Society of Forensic Odontology
 (ASFO)
http://www.asfo.org

Armed Forces Institute of Pathology (AFIP)
6825 16th Street N.W.
Washington, DC 20306–6000
202–782–2100
http://www.afip.org

Armed Forces Institute of Pathology (AFIP)
Armed Forces DNA Identification
 Laboratory (AFDIL)
Department of Defense DNA Registry
1413 Research Boulevard
Building 101, Second Floor
Rockville, MD 20850–3125
301–319–0000
http://www.afip.org/Departments/
 oafme/dna

Armed Forces Institute of Pathology (AFIP)
Department of Oral and Maxillofacial
 Pathology
6825 16th Street N.W.
Room 3096
Washington, DC 20306–6000
202–782–1800
http://www.afip.org/Departments/
 OMaxPath2/index.html

Armed Forces Institute of Pathology (AFIP)
Office of the Armed Forces Medical
 Examiner (OAFME)
AFIP/OAFME, AFIP Annex
1413 Research Boulevard
Building 102
Rockville, MD 20850
800–944–7912 or 301–319–0000
http://www.afip.org/Departments/oafme

American Society of Crime Laboratory
 Directors (ASCLD)
P.O. Box 2710
Largo, FL 33779
727–541–2982
http://www.ascld.org

American Society of Crime Laboratory
 Directors/Laboratory Accreditation Board
 (ASCLD/LAB)
139 J Technology Drive
Garner, NC 27529
919–773–2600
http://www.ascld-lab.org

Centers for Disease Control and
 Prevention (CDC)
1600 Clifton Road
Atlanta, GA 30333
800–311–3435 or 404–639–3534
http://www.cdc.gov

Chemical Transportation Emergency
 Center (CHEMTREC)
1300 Wilson Boulevard
Arlington, VA 22209
703–741–5525
http://www.chemtrec.org

Disaster Mortuary Operational Response
 Team (DMORT)
http://www.dmort.org

DMORT Victim Identification Program (VIP)
VIP@DMORT.org

Federal Aviation Administration (FAA)
800 Independence Avenue S.W.
Room 810
Washington, DC 20591
http://www.faa.gov

Federal Bureau of Investigation (FBI)
J. Edgar Hoover Building
935 Pennsylvania Avenue N.W.
Washington, DC 20535–0001
202–324–3000
http://www.fbi.gov

FBI Critical Incident Response Group
(CIRG)
http://www.fbi.gov/hq/isd/cirg/
mission.htm

FBI Disaster Squad
http://www.fbi.gov/hq/lab/disaster/
disaster.htm

FBI Evidence Response Team (ERT)
http://www.fbi.gov/hq/lab/ert/ertmain.htm

FBI Hazardous Materials Response Unit
http://www.fbi.gov/hq/lab/org/hmru.htm

FBI Laboratory
http://www.fbi.gov/hq/lab/labhome.htm

FBI Laboratory Services
http://www.fbi.gov/hq/lab/org/labchart.htm

Federal Emergency Management Agency
(FEMA)
500 C Street S.W.
Washington, DC 20472
202–566–1600
http://www.fema.gov

FEMA National Urban Search and Rescue
(US&R) Response System
http://www.fema.gov/usr

International Association of Coroners and
Medical Examiners (IACME)
P.O. Box 44834
Columbus, OH 43204–0834
614–276–8384

International Association of Identification
(IAI)
2535 Pilot Knob Road
Suite 117
Mendota Heights, MN 55120–1120
651–681–8566
http://www.theiai.org

International Police Criminal Organization
(Interpol)
200 quai Charles de Gaulle
69006 Lyon, France
Fax: (33) 4 72 44 71 63
http://www.interpol.com

Interpol Disaster Victim Identification (DVI)
Guide
http://www.interpol.com/Public/
DisasterVictim/Guide

Interpol Disaster Victim Identification (DVI)
Forms
http://www.interpol.com/Public/
DisasterVictim/Forms

National Association of Counties (NACO)
440 First Street N.W.
Suite 800
Washington, DC 20001
202–393–6226
http://www.naco.org

National Association of Medical Examiners
(NAME)
430 Pryor Street S.W.
Atlanta, GA 30312
404–730–4781
http://www.thename.org

National Guard Bureau
1411 Jefferson Davis Highway
Arlington, VA 22202–3231
703–607–3162
http://www.ngb.army.mil

Air National Guard Readiness Center
3500 Fetchet Avenue
Andrews AFB, MD 20762–5157

Army National Guard Readiness Center
111 South George Mason Drive
Arlington, VA 22204

National Center for Forensic Science
(NCFS)
University of Central Florida
P.O. Box 162367
Orlando, FL 32816
407–823–6469
http://www.ncfs.org

National Forensic Science Technology
Center (NFSTC)
7881 114th Avenue North
Largo, FL 33773
727–549–6067
http://www.nfstc.org

National Transportation Safety Board
(NTSB)
490 L'Enfant Plaza S.W.
Washington, DC 20594
202–314–6000
http://www.ntsb.gov

Occupational Safety and Health
Administration (OSHA)
200 Constitution Avenue N.W.
Washington, DC 20210
http://www.osha.gov

Royal Canadian Mounted Police (RCMP)
http://www.rcmp-grc.gc.ca

U.S. Army Central Identification
Laboratory, Hawaii (CILHI) [now Joint
POW/MIA Accounting Command]
310 Worchester Avenue
Building 45
Hickam AFB, HI 96853–5530
808–448–8903
http://www.cilhi.army.mil

U.S. Department of Energy (DOE)
1000 Independence Avenue S.W.
Washington, DC 20585
800–DIAL–DOE (342–5363)
http://www.energy.gov

U.S. Department of Homeland Security
Federal Emergency Management Agency
National Disaster Medical System (NDMS)
Section
500 C Street S.W.
Suite 713
Washington, DC 20472
800–USA–NDMS (872–6367)
http://ndms.dhhs.gov

U.S. Department of Homeland Security
Office for Domestic Preparedness
810 Seventh Street N.W.
Washington, DC 20531
800–368–6498
http://www.ojp.usdoj.gov/odp

U.S. Department of Justice
Office for Victims of Crime
Victim Assistance Center
810 Seventh Street N.W.
Washington, DC 20531
800–627–6872
http://www.ojp.usdoj.gov/ovc

U.S. Department of Transportation
400 Seventh Street S.W.
Washington, DC 20590
202–366–4000
http://www.dot.gov

U.S. Environmental Protection Agency
(EPA)
Ariel Rios Building
1200 Pennsylvania Avenue N.W.
Washington, DC 20460
202–272–0167
http://www.epa.gov

WinID (Dental Computer System)
http://www.winid.com

Appendix B. Disaster Mortuary Operational Response Team Activation

The Disaster Mortuary Operational Response Team (DMORT) is a federally funded team of forensic and mortuary personnel experienced in disaster victim identification. DMORT provides a mobile morgue, victim identification and tracking software, and specific personnel to augment local resources. DMORT is part of the National Disaster Medical System, a section of the U.S. Department of Homeland Security, Federal Emergency Management Agency (FEMA).

DMORT can be activated by one of four methods:

Federal Disaster Declaration. The *Federal Response Plan* dictates how Federal agencies respond following a disaster. A request for DMORT assistance must be made by a local official through the State emergency management agency, which will then contact the regional office of FEMA. Based on the severity of the disaster, FEMA can ask for a Presidential disaster declaration, allowing the DMORT team to be activated. This process can take from 24 to 48 hours.

Aviation Disaster Family Assistance Act. Under this Federal act, the National Transportation Safety Board (NTSB) can ask for DMORT's assistance. The act covers most passenger aircraft accidents in the United States and U.S. territories. NTSB coordinates with the local medicolegal authority to assess local resources and capabilities and can activate DMORT on the request of the local authority.

Public Health Act. Under this Act, the U.S. Public Health Service can provide support to a State or locality that cannot provide the necessary response. However, the State or locality must pay for DMORT's services, including salary, expenses, and other costs.

Memorandum of Understanding (MOU) with Federal Agency. A Federal agency may request that DMORT provide disaster victim identification. Under this mechanism, the requesting agency must pay the cost of the DMORT deployment. As an example, following the crash of United Airlines Flight 93 in Pennsylvania on September 11, 2001, DMORT was activated under an MOU with the FBI.

Other DMORT issues include the following:

- DMORT normally requires 24 to 48 hours to become fully operational.

- The DMORT portable morgue requires a building for morgue operations. This guide lists potential disaster morgue sites capable of housing the DMORT morgue (see p. 6).

- The Federal Government pays travel, lodging, food, salary, and other expenses of DMORT personnel, except in the case of an activation under the Public Health Act.

- The DMORT team supports the local medicolegal authority by providing expertise, personnel, supplies, and equipment. The responsibility for assigning the cause and manner of death, signing of death certificates, and death notification remain with the local authority. All records created by DMORT should be left with the local authority. DMORT should provide identification reports and a computer program documenting the information collected during their response.

- The DMORT family assistance center (FAC) team assists in the organization and operation of the FAC.

- If a DMORT team member is activated from your agency to work at a disaster, that employee should present you with a copy of his or her travel orders as proof of activation.

Appendix C. Facilities/Organizational Flow Chart

Exhibit C–1. **Identification Flow Chart***

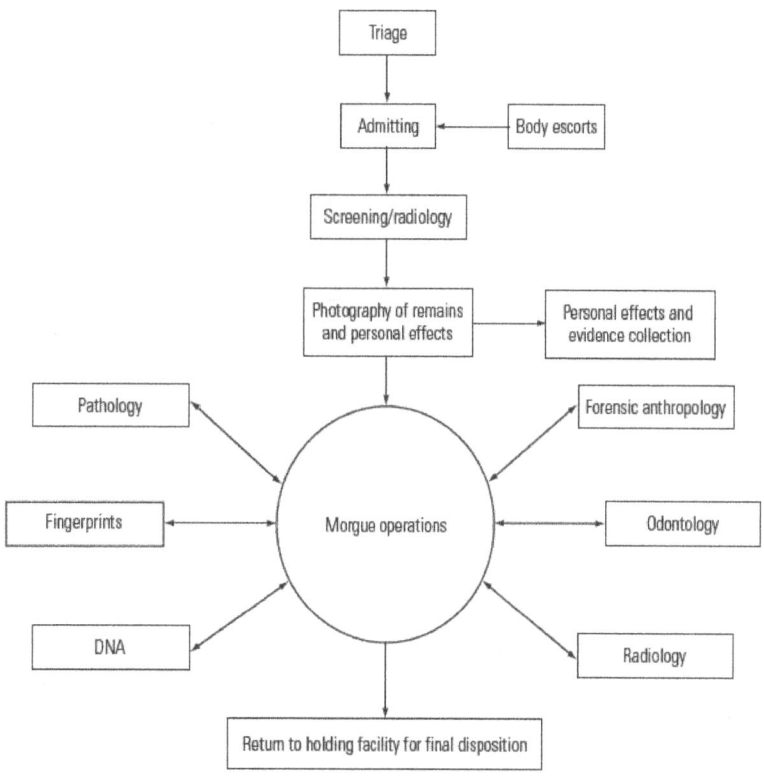

*The following represents only a suggested model; this process may vary according to local circumstances.

Exhibit C–2. Forensic Information Management and Coordination*

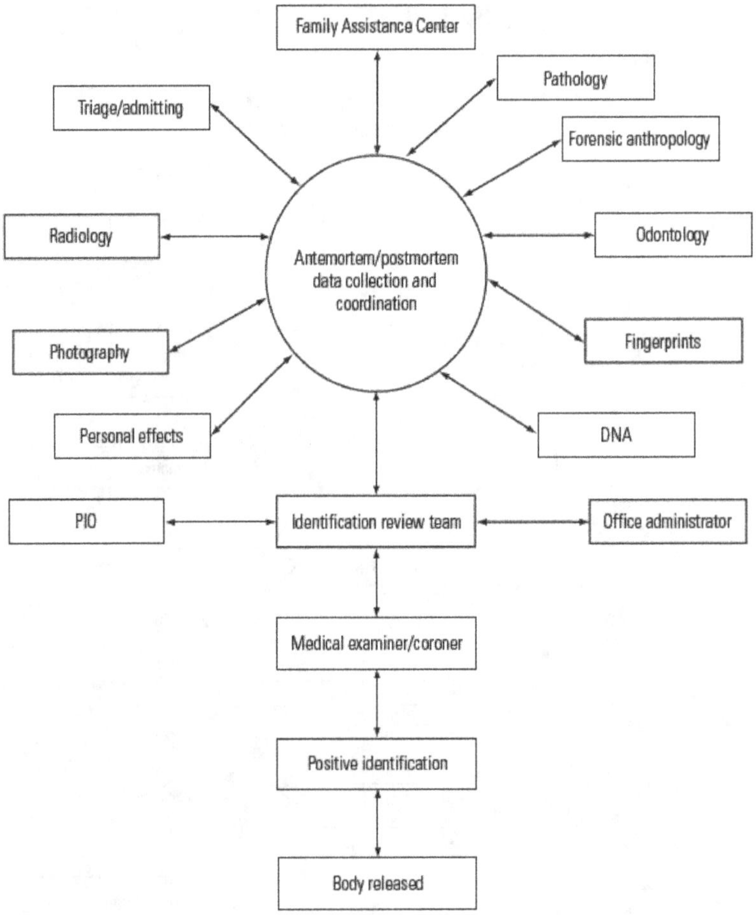

*The following represents only a suggested model; this process may vary according to local circumstances.

Appendix D. Procedures for DNA Sample Collection

The DNA sample team works in pairs: a recorder and a sampler. The recorder escorts the remains to the worktable. Both team members verify (or establish) unique identifiers and mutually acknowledge a site for sampling (if a decision is made *not* to sample the remains, the recorder notes that in the DNA Remains Tracking Log).

The recorder enters the number, date, time, and description into a database or log and labels the specimen container (e.g., tube, bag, etc.) appropriately.

Using the appropriate instruments, the sampler obtains one of the following, listed in order of preference:

- 10–15 g of deep skeletal muscle (avoid tissues that may have been crushed together by incident impact or blast forces).

- 1–2 cm x 4–6 cm x 0.5–1 cm of cortical bone (avoid anthropological landmarks, articular margins, and fresh-broken margins whenever possible; cut windows in long bones and crania).

- Upper or lower canine or other intact tooth without restorations (consult an odontologist if required).

- Other portion of soft or hard tissue that fits into a 50 ml conical tube.

The recorder and sampler verify the placement of the sample in a properly labeled tube and the entry of the corresponding data in a sample log. The sampler disposes of the bench coat, scalpel blades, and rotary bits. The sampler cleans the cutting surface, scale, Stryker saw, rotary instrument, forceps, gloves, and hemostats with a 10-percent bleach solution, then wipes all surfaces down with ethanol.

The medical examiner/coroner is expected to provide guidance to the DNA sample team regarding tissue samples that are likely to be exhausted during testing.

If multiple, potentially unassociated remains are in a single recovery container, the recorder or sampler is expected to separately bag the remains from which the sample was taken. Later, when DNA results are obtained, the medical examiner/coroner is expected to be able to return to that recovery container and attribute that profile to a specific tissue specimen with certainty.

The chain of custody is expected to list all samples sent to the laboratory facility. On signing the chain of custody, the medical examiner/coroner is also expected to decide whether to return any remaining soft tissue or osseous sample after testing is completed. Because single, recovered teeth are submitted whole, consider how to return them after testing is completed.

Appendix E. DNA Sample Family Reference Collection Forms

Donor Information

Last Name		First Name				Middle Name
Social Security Number (if applicable)				Home Telephone Number		
Home Street Address						
City		State		ZIP		Country
Date of Birth (Month/Day/Year)						

Family Relationship
Please circle your kinship to the missing individual.

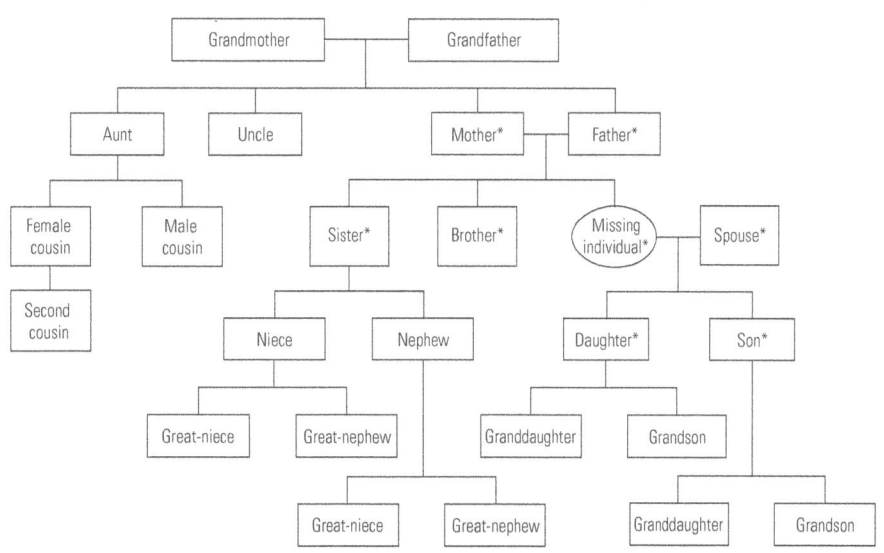

Missing Individual Information

Last Name		First Name		Middle Name
Date of Birth (Month/Day/Year)		Social Security Number (if applicable)		

---

*Primary donor for a nuclear DNA reference (see list of primary donors on p.64).

Potential Living Biological Donors

Mother/Father of Missing Individual

Name	Age	Address	Phone

Brothers/Sisters of Missing Individual

Name	Age	Address	Phone

Spouse of Missing Individual

Name	Age	Address	Phone

Children of Missing Individual

Name	Age	Address	Phone

Primary Donor for Nuclear DNA Analysis

An appropriate family member for nuclear DNA analysis is someone who is biologically related to and only one generation removed from the deceased. The following are the family members who are appropriate donors to provide reference specimens, in the order of preference:

1. Natural (biological) mother *and* father, *or*

2. Spouse *and* natural (biological) children, *or*

3. Natural (biological) mother or father and victim's biological children, *or*

4. Multiple full siblings of the victim (i.e., children from the same mother and father).

Sample Donor Consent Form

Note: This form is a sample only based on forms developed by the Armed Forces for the DOD DNA registry. The law concerning DNA samples varies across jurisdictions. Modify forms accordingly.

PRIVACY ACT STATEMENT/STATEMENT OF CONSENT

AUTHORITY: 5 U.S.C. 301; 10 U.S.C. 3012; Pub. L. 91–121, Section 404 (a) (2); and memo dated 16 December 1991 from Deputy Secretary of Defense, Subject: DOD DNA Registry. Also under authority of 10 U.S.C. 176 and 177, Pub. L. 94–361; DOD Directive 5154.23; and, if Social Security number collected, EO 9397.

PRINCIPAL PURPOSE(S): Establish a DNA reference specimen repository and database of information from kindred family members of unaccounted for/unidentified service members or other individuals who need to be identified. DNA will be extracted from either vials of blood, dried blood, and/or oral swabs, and will be used in identifying human remains.

ROUTINE USE(S): None.

DISCLOSURE: Voluntary. Failure to provide reference sample or information may render DNA identification impossible.

STATEMENT OF CONSENT

The above answers are correct to the best of my knowledge and belief, and I understand that my answers are important in determining my kindred family relationship to an unaccounted for service member or other unaccounted for individual. I have also read the Privacy Act statement above.

Realizing that nuclear or mitochondrial deoxyribonucleic acid (DNA) may be extracted from my blood and used in the identification of a kindred family member, I agree to donate my blood, to have my DNA analyzed if necessary, and to have my name and other relevant typing information placed in a confidential registry or database for identification and statistical analysis.

I am voluntarily donating tubes of blood via venipuncture, or if impracticable, consenting to the fingerstick method of securing a small amount of blood, or allowing the taking of an oral swab.

I have not received a blood transfusion within the last 3 months (if you have received a transfusion, please wait for a period of 90 days following the transfusion before providing the reference sample).

I consent to the Armed Forces using the information and specimens for the identification of any unaccounted for family members.

_____   _____   _____

Signature of Donor   **Printed Name of Donor**   **Date**

VERIFICATION OF DONOR IDENTIFICATION AND SPECIMEN COLLECTION

I have verified from a photo ID that the blood or other biological specimen collected has come from the above-stated donor, and have confirmed the donor's name and/or Social Security number placed on the collection tubes.

_____   _____   _____

Signature of Collector   **Printed Name of Collector**   **Date**

Appendix F. Dental Numbering System

Exhibit F–1. Dental Nomenclature Conversion Table: Deciduous Teeth (Revised)[a]

Deciduous			Upper right					Upper left		
System/tooth[b]	2M	1M	C	I2	I1	I1	I2	C	1M	2M
Universal	A	B	C	D	E	F	G	H	I	J
Palmer	E+	D+	C+	B+	A+	+A	+B	+C	+D	+E
FDI	55	54	53	52	51	61	62	63	64	65
Hareup	05+	04+	03+	02+	01+	+01	+02	+03	+04	+05
Other	V	IV	III	II	I	I	II	III	IV	V
Other	5D	4D	3D	2D	1D	1D	2D	3D	4D	5D
Other	d5	d4	d3	d2	d1	d1	d2	d3	d4	d5
Other	5m	4m	3m	2m	1m	1m	2m	3m	4m	5m
Other	A	B	C	D	E	E	D	C	B	A
Other	dm2	dm1	dc	di2	di1	di1	di2	dc	dm1	dm2
FDI Modified	55	54	53	52	51	61	62	63	64	65

			Lower right					Lower left		
	2M	1M	C	I2	I1	I1	I2	C	1M	2M
Universal	T	S	R	Q	P	O	N	M	L	K
Palmer	E-	D-	C-	B-	A-	-A	-B	-C	-D	-E
FDI	85	84	83	82	81	71	72	73	74	75
Hareup	05-	04-	03-	02-	01-	-01	-02	-03	-04	-05
Other	V	IV	III	II	I	I	II	III	IV	V
Other	5D	4D	3D	2D	1D	1D	2D	3D	4D	5D
Other	d5	d4	d3	d2	d1	d1	d2	d3	d4	d5
Other	5m	4m	3m	2m	1m	1m	2m	3m	4m	5m
Other	A	B	C	D	E	E	D	C	B	A
Other	dm2	dm1	dc	di2	di1	di1	di2	dc	dm1	dm2
FDI Modified	75	74	73	72	71	81	82	83	84	85

---

[a]Compiled by Robert Dorion, D.D.S., Diplomate of the American Board of Forensic Odontology. Reprinted from Bowers, C. Michael, and Gary Bell, eds., *Manual of Forensic Odonotology,* 3d ed., American Society of Forensic Odontology, 1995.

[b]2M=second molar; 1M=first molar; C=cuspid; I2=second incisor (lateral incisor); I1=first incisor (central incisor)

Exhibit F–2. Dental Nomenclature Conversion Table: Permanent Teeth—Upper (Revised)[a]

Permanent System/tooth[b]	Upper right								Upper left							
	3M	2M	1M	2P	1P	C	I2	I1	I1	I2	C	1P	2P	1M	2M	3M
Other	UR8	UR7	UR6	UR5	UR4	UR3	UR2	UR1	UL1	UL2	UL3	UL4	UL5	UL6	UL7	UL8
Hareup	8+	7+	6+	5+	4+	3+	2+	1+	+1	+2	+3	+4	+5	+6	+7	+8
Palmer	8⌋	7⌋	6⌋	5⌋	4⌋	3⌋	2⌋	1⌋	⌊1	⌊2	⌊3	⌊4	⌊5	⌊6	⌊7	⌊8
Universal	1	2	3	4	5	6	7	8	9	10	11	12	13	14	15	16
FDI	18	17	16	15	14	13	12	11	21	22	23	24	25	26	27	28
Bosworth	8	7	6	5	4	3	2	1	1	2	3	4	5	6	7	8
Lowlands	M3	M2	M1	P2	P1	C	I2	I1	I1	I2	C	P1	P2	M1	M2	M3
Europe	D8	D7	D6	D5	D4	D3	D2	D1	G1	G2	G3	G4	G5	G6	G7	G8
Holland	sdM3	sdM2	sdM1	sdP2	sdP1	sdC	sdI2	sdI1	sgI1	sgI2	sgC	sgP1	sgP2	sgM1	sgM2	sgM3
FDI Modified	18	17	16	15	14	13	12	11	21	22	23	24	25	26	27	28
Other	16	15	14	13	12	11	10	9	8	7	6	5	4	3	2	1

[a] Compiled by Robert Dorion, D.D.S., Diplomate of the American Board of Forensic Odontology. Reprinted from Bowers, C. Michael, and Gary Bell, eds., *Manual of Forensic Odontology*, 3d ed., American Society of Forensic Odontology, 1995.

[b] 3M=third molar; 2M=second molar; 1M=first molar; 2P=second premolar; 1P=first premolar; C=cuspid; I2=second incisor (lateral incisor), I1=first incisor (central incisor)

Exhibit F–3. Dental Nomenclature Conversion Table: Permanent Teeth—Lower (Revised)[a]

Permanent System/tooth[b]	Lower right								Lower left							
	3M	2M	1M	2P	1P	C	I2	I1	I1	I2	C	1P	2P	1M	2M	3M
Other	LR8	LR7	LR6	LR5	LR4	LR3	LR2	LR1	LL1	LL2	LL3	LL4	LL5	LL6	LL7	LL8
Hareup	8-	7-	6-	5-	4-	3-	2-	1-	-1	-2	-3	-4	-5	-6	-7	-8
Palmer	8⌉	7⌉	6⌉	5⌉	4⌉	3⌉	2⌉	1⌉	⌈1	⌈2	⌈3	⌈4	⌈5	⌈6	⌈7	⌈8
Universal	32	31	30	29	28	27	26	25	24	23	22	21	20	19	18	17
FDI	48	47	46	45	44	43	42	41	31	32	33	34	35	36	37	38
Bosworth	H	G	F	E	D	C	B	A	A	B	C	D	E	F	G	H
Lowlands	M3	M2	M1	P2	P1	C	I2	I1	I1	I2	C	P1	P2	M1	M2	M3
Europe	d8	d7	d6	d5	d4	d3	d2	d1	g1	g2	g3	g4	g5	g6	g7	g8
Holland	diM3	diM2	diM1	diP2	diP1	diC	diI2	diI1	giI1	giI2	giC	giP1	giP2	giM1	giM2	giM3
FDI Modified	38	37	36	35	34	33	32	31	41	42	43	44	45	46	47	48
Other	32	31	30	29	28	27	26	25	24	23	22	21	20	19	18	17

[a] Compiled by Robert Dorion, D.D.S., Diplomate of the American Board of Forensic Odontology. Reprinted from Bowers, C. Michael, and Gary Bell, eds., *Manual of Forensic Odontology*, 3d ed., American Society of Forensic Odontology, 1995.

[b] 3M=third molar; 2M=second molar; 1M=first molar; 2P=second premolar; 1P=first premolar; C=cuspid; I2=second incisor (lateral incisor), I1=first incisor (central incisor)

Appendix G. Sample Remains Release Authorization Form

Release Authorization

Name of Deceased: _____

Please be advised that identified human tissue will be buried in an appropriate manner.

In the event any additional tissue(s) are recovered in the future and are identified as belonging to the above named deceased, **I/WE** request the following (please check **ONE** of the boxes below):

❏ **I/WE** do not wish to be notified. **I/WE** are authorizing the appropriate administrator(s) to dispose of said tissue(s) by methods deemed appropriate by said administrator(s).

❏ **I/WE** wish to be notified and will make a decision regarding disposition at that time.

I/WE the undersigned hereby authorize _____ to release the
                                          (Name of Medical Examiner/Coroner)

remains of _____ to the designated Disaster Mortuary Operational
              (Name of Deceased)

Response Team (DMORT).

I/WE further authorize the designated DMORT to embalm, perform postmortem reconstructive surgery techniques, and otherwise prepare the remains as they deem necessary, and on completion to release the remains to

_____

(Name, Address, and Phone No. of Funeral Home/Agent).

I/WE certify that **I/WE** have read and understand this **RELEASE AUTHORIZATION. I/WE** further state **I/WE** are all of the next of kin or represent all of the next of kin and am/are legally authorized and/or charged with the responsibility of burial and/or final disposition of above said deceased.

Signed _____ Relationship to Deceased _____

Print Name _____ Date Signed _____ Time _____

Complete Address _____

Telephone Number _____

Signed _____ Relationship to Deceased _____

Print Name _____ Date Signed _____ Time _____

Complete Address _____

Telephone Number _____

Witness _____

Print Witness Name _____

List of Reviewers

Academy of General Dentistry

Academy of Radiology Research

Air National Guard Readiness Center (Andrews AFB, Maryland)

Alabama Emergency Management Agency

Alaska Dental Society

Alaska Division of Emergency Services

American Academy of Experts in Traumatic Stress

American Academy of Forensic Psychology

American Academy of Forensic Sciences

American Academy of Oral and Maxillofacial Pathology

American Association of Dental Examiners

American Association of Oral and Maxillofacial Surgeons

American Bar Association

American Board of Criminalistics

American Board of Emergency Medicine

American Board of Examiners in Crisis Intervention

American Board of Forensic Anthropology

American Board of Forensic Toxicology

American Board of Medical Specialties

American Board of Medicolegal Death Investigators

American Board of Nuclear Medicine

American Board of Oral and Maxillofacial Radiology

American Board of Pathology

American Board of Radiology

American College of Emergency Physicians

American College of Forensic Examiners

American College of Radiology

American Dental Association

American Medical Association

American Society of Crime Laboratory Directors

American Society of Forensic Odontology

American Society of Law Enforcement Trainers

Arapahoe County Sheriff's Office (Littleton, Colorado)

Arizona Department of Health Services, Bureau of State Lab Services

Arizona Department of Public Safety

Arizona Division of Emergency Management

Arkansas Department of Emergency Management

Arlington County Sheriff's Office (Virginia)

Arlington Professional Firefighters and Paramedics Association (Virginia)

Armed Forces Institute of Pathology (AFIP)

AFIP, Department of Oral and Maxillofacial Pathology

AFIP, Office of the Armed Forces Medical Examiner (OAFME)

AFIP, OAFME, Department of Defense DNA Registry

AFIP, OAFME, Department of Legal Medicine

Armed Forces Radiobiology Research Institute

Army National Guard Readiness Center (Arlington, Virginia)

Association of Federal Defense Attorneys

Association of Forensic DNA Analysts and Administrators

Baptist Hospital East, Radiation Department (Louisville, Kentucky)

Bexar County Forensic Science Center (San Antonio, Texas)

Bode Technology Group, Inc.

Broward County Sheriff's Office (Fort Lauderdale, Florida)

Bureau of Legal Dentistry (Vancouver, British Columbia)

C.A. Pound Human Identification Lab, University of Florida

California Criminalistics Institute

California Dental Association

California Department of Justice, Bureau of Forensic Services

California Department of Justice, DNA Laboratory

California State University, Center for Hazards Research

California State University, Department of Anthropology

Camden Police Department (Delaware)

Canadian Centre for Emergency Preparedness

Canadian Society of Forensic Science

Carnegie Mellon University

Celera Genomics

Centers for Disease Control and Prevention

City of Boston Office of the Chief Medical Examiner (Massachusetts)

City of Casselberry Police Department (Florida)

City of Cleveland Heights Police Department (Ohio)

City of Detroit Office of the Chief Medical Examiner (Michigan)

City of Honolulu Department of the Medical Examiner (Hawaii)

City of New York Office of the Chief Medical Examiner (New York)

City of Richmond Office of the Chief Medical Examiner (Virginia)

City of San Diego Office of the Medical Examiner (California)

College of American Pathologists

College of Mount St. Joseph, Department of Biology

Colorado Bureau of Investigation

Colorado College, Department of Anthropology

Colorado Dental Association

Colorado Emergency Management Association

Colorado Office of Emergency Management

Colorado State University

Commission of Accreditation for Law Enforcement Agencies

Connecticut Department of Public Safety

Connecticut Office of Emergency Management

Connecticut State Dental Association

Connecticut State Police Forensic Laboratory

Cook County Hospital, Radiology Department (Chicago, Illinois)

Cook County Medical Examiner's Office (Chicago, Illinois)

Cook County Public Defender's Office (Chicago, Illinois)

Council of State Governments

Delaware Department of Public Safety

Delaware Emergency Management Agency

Delaware Office of the Chief Medical Examiner (Wilmington, Delaware)

Department of the Army, United States Army Criminal Investigation Laboratory

Disaster Recovery Institute International (Falls Church, Virginia)

Disaster Research Center (Newark, Delaware)

District of Columbia Emergency Management Agency

Dover Air Force Base (Dover, Delaware)

Dupage County Coroner's Office (Park Ridge, Illinois)

Emergency Response and Research Institute

Federal Aviation Administration

Federal Bureau of Investigation

Federal Emergency Management Agency

Federal Law Enforcement Training Center

First Special Response Group (Moffett Field, California)

Florida City and County Management Association

Florida Dental Association

Florida Department of Law Enforcement

Florida Division of Emergency Management

Florida Highway Patrol

Florida Society of Oral and Maxillofacial Surgeons

Forensic Association of Philadelphia (Pennsylvania)

Fulton County Medical Examiner's Center (Atlanta, Georgia)

Georgia Bureau of Investigation

Georgia Emergency Management Agency

Hawaii State Voluntary Organizations Active in Disaster

Idaho Bureau of Disaster Services

Illinois Emergency Management Agency

Illinois State Police, Division of Forensic Science

Indiana Coroners Association

Indiana State Emergency Management Agency

Indiana State Police

Indiana University Medical Center

Indiana University School of Dentistry

Institute for Law and Justice (Alexandria, Virginia)

International Association for Identification

International Association for Identification, Arizona Division

International Association for Identification, Chesapeake Bay Division

International Association for Identification, Florida Division

International Association for Identification, Georgia Division

International Association for Identification, Illinois Division

International Association for Identification, Iowa Division

International Association for Identification, New Jersey Division

International Association of Chiefs of Police

International Association of Emergency Managers

International Association of Fire Chiefs

International City/County Managers Association

International Commission on Missing Persons (Sarajevo, Bosnia-Herzegovina)

International Critical Incident Stress Foundation

International Police Criminal Organization (Lyon, France)

International/American Association for Dental Research

Iowa Emergency Management Division

Iowa State Office of the Medical Examiner, Iowa Department of Public Health

Jefferson County Sheriff's Office (Golden, Colorado)

Kansas Division of Emergency Management

Kansas Voluntary Organizations Active in Disasters

Kentucky Division of Emergency Management

Kentucky Voluntary Organizations Active in Disasters

Kenyon International Emergency Services, Inc.

Los Angeles County Sheriff's Office (California)

Louisiana Dental Association

Louisiana Office of Emergency Preparedness

Louisiana State Coroners Association

Louisiana State University School of Dentistry

Lucas County Coroner's Office (Toledo, Ohio)

Maine Department of Defense, Veterans, and Emergency Management

Marshall University, Forensic Science Center

Maryland Emergency Management Agency

Maryland State Dental Association

Maryland Voluntary Organizations Active in Disasters

Massachusetts Dental Society

Massachusetts Emergency Management Agency

Massachusetts Executive Office of Public Safety

Massachusetts State Police

Massachusetts State Police Crime Laboratory

Medical College of Virginia

Mercyhurst Archaeological Institute, Mercyhurst College

Miami-Dade County Fire Rescue Department (Miami, Florida)

Miami-Dade County Medical Examiner's Office (Miami, Florida)

Miami-Dade County Police Department, Crime Laboratory Bureau (Miami, Florida)

Miami-Dade County Police Department, Criminal Investigations Division (Miami, Florida)

Miami-Dade County Voluntary Organizations Active in Disasters

Michigan State University, Department of Anthropology

Mid-Atlantic Association of Forensic Scientists

Midwestern Association of Forensic Scientists

Milwaukee County Medical Examiner's Office (Milwaukee, Wisconsin)

Minnesota Department of Public Safety

Minnesota Division of Emergency Management

Minnesota Voluntary Organizations Active in Disasters

Mississippi Crime Laboratory

Mississippi Emergency Management Agency

Missouri State Emergency Management Agency

Montana Disaster and Emergency Services

Myriad Genetics, Inc.

National Association of Counties

National Association of Criminal Defense Lawyers

National Association of Medical Examiners

National Association of Police Organizations

National Center for Forensic Science

National Center for Post Traumatic Stress Disorders

National Disaster Medical System

National District Attorneys Association

National DNA Data Bank of Canada

National Emergency Management Association

National Emergency Response Team

National Forensic Science Technology Center

National Governors Association

National Guard Bureau

National Institute for Urban Search and Rescue (Santa Barbara, California)

National Institute of Dental and Craniofacial Research

National Institutes of Health

National Law Enforcement Council

National League of Cities

National Legal Aid and Defender Association

National Museum of Health and Medicine

National Search and Rescue School (Yorktown, Virginia)

National Sheriffs' Association

National Transportation Safety Board

National Transportation Safety Board, Office of Family Affairs

National Voluntary Organizations Active in Disaster

Natural Hazards Center (Boulder, Colorado)

Naval Dental Research Institute (Great Lakes, Illinois)

Nevada Division of Emergency Management

New Jersey Dental Association

New Jersey Department of Law and Public Safety

New Jersey State Police

New Mexico Emergency Management Bureau

New York City Police Department

New York City Voluntary Organizations Active in Disaster

New York State Division of Criminal Justice Services

New York State Emergency Management Office

New York State Police Crime Laboratory

New York State Voluntary Organizations Active in Disasters

North Carolina Dental Society

North Carolina Department of Crime Control and Public Safety

North Carolina Division of Emergency Management

North Carolina Office of the Chief Medical Examiner (Chapel Hill, North Carolina)

North Carolina State Board of Dental Examiners

North Dakota Emergency Management

Northeastern Association of Forensic Scientists

Occupational Safety and Health Administration, U.S. Department of Labor

Office of Critical Infrastructure Protection and Emergency Preparedness (Ontario, Canada)

Office of Emergency Preparedness, U.S. Department of Health and Human Services

Ohio Dental Association

Ohio Department of Public Safety

Ohio State Coroners Association

Oklahoma Department of Civil Emergency Management

Oklahoma State Office of the Chief Medical Examiner

Oklahoma Voluntary Organizations Active in Disasters

Onondaga County Center for Forensic Sciences (Syracuse, New York)

Orange County Fire and Rescue Department (Winter Park, Florida)

Oregon Emergency Management

Oregon State Police, Medical Examiners Division

Pennsylvania Dental Association

Pennsylvania Emergency Management Agency Eastern, Central, and Western Region Offices

Pennsylvania Voluntary Organizations Active in Disasters

Province of Alberta Office of the Chief Examiner (Edmonton, Canada)

Province of Ontario Chief Coroner's Office (Toronto, Canada)

Province of Ontario Dental Identification Team (Canada)

Pulaski County Coroner's Office (Little Rock, Arkansas)

Rhode Island Dental Association

Rhode Island Emergency Management Agency

Rhode Island Office of the Chief Medical Examiner

Royal Canadian Mounted Police

RPI/Titan Corporation

Saint Louis University School of Medicine

Sandia National Laboratories

Search and Rescue Council of New Jersey

Simon Fraser University, Department of Archaeology

Smithsonian Institution Department of Anthropology, National Museum of Natural History

Society of Forensic Toxicologists

Society of Nuclear Medicine

Society of Skeletal Radiology

South Carolina Emergency Management Division

South Dakota Division of Emergency Management

Southern Association of Forensic Scientists

Southern California Association of Fingerprint Officers

Southern Institute for Forensic Science

Southwest Texas State University, Department of Anthropology

Southwestern Association of Forensic Scientists

St. Louis County Medical Examiner's Office (St. Louis, Missouri)

Suffolk County Crime Laboratory (Hauppauge, New York)

Suffolk County Dental Society (New York)

Suffolk County Fire, Rescue, and Emergency Services (New York)

Suffolk County Medical Examiner's Office (Hauppauge, New York)

Tarrant County Medical Examiner's Office (Fort Worth, Texas)

Tennessee Emergency Management Agency

Texas Department of Public Safety

Transportation Safety Board of Canada

Tulsa Police Department (Tulsa, Oklahoma)

U.S. Air Force Dental Investigation Service

U.S. Air Force Rescue Coordination Center

U.S. Army Central Identification Laboratory (Hickam AFB, Hawaii) [now Joint POW/MIA Accounting Command]

U.S. Conference of Mayors

U.S. Department of Transportation

U.S. Environmental Protection Agency

University of California (Los Angeles), Center for Public Health and Disasters

University of California (Santa Cruz)

University of Central Florida, Department of Chemistry

University of Central Florida, Institute for Simulation and Training

University of Colorado School of Dentistry

University of Detroit, Mercy Institute for Advanced Continuing Dental Education

University of Hawaii, Department of Anthropology

University of Illinois, Anthropology Department

University of Indianapolis, Biology Department

University of New Mexico, Department of Anthropology

University of New Mexico School of Medicine

University of North Carolina, Department of Sociology/Anthropology

University of North Dakota, Department of Anthropology

University of North Florida, Institute of Police Technology and Management

University of North Texas, Laboratory of Forensic Anthropology and Human Identification

University of North Texas Police Academy

University of South Alabama Medical Center, Department of Radiology

University of South Carolina, Department of Anthropology

University of Tennessee, Department of Anthropology

University of Toronto, Forensic Science/Forensic Anthropology

University of Washington, Radiology Department

University of Wyoming, Department of Anthropology

Utah Department of Public Safety

Ventura County Coroner's Office (California)

Ventura County Sheriff's Office of Emergency Services (California)

Vermont Emergency Management

Vermont Forensic Laboratory

Victorian Institute of Forensic Medicine (Australia)

Virginia Dental Association

Virginia Department of Emergency
Management

Virginia Institute of Forensic Science and
Medicine

Virginia Voluntary Organizations Active in
Disasters

Volusia County Fire Services (Deland,
Florida)

Wake County District Attorney's Office
(Raleigh, North Carolina)

Washington Voluntary Organizations Active
in Disasters

Washoe County Sheriff's Office (Reno,
Nevada)

Wayne County Medical Examiner's Office
(Detroit, Michigan)

West Virginia Office of Emergency
Services

West Virginia Office of the Chief Medical
Examiner Office (South Charleston,
West Virginia)

West Virginia University, Forensic
Identification Program

Western Michigan University, Department
of Anthropology

Wisconsin Association for Identification

Wisconsin Emergency Management

Wisconsin State Historical Society

Wyoming Emergency Management
Agency

About the National Institute of Justice

NIJ is the research, development, and evaluation agency of the U.S. Department of Justice. The Institute provides objective, independent, evidence-based knowledge and tools to enhance the administration of justice and public safety. NIJ's principal authorities are derived from the Omnibus Crime Control and Safe Streets Act of 1968, as amended (see 42 U.S.C. §§ 3721–3723).

The NIJ Director is appointed by the President and confirmed by the Senate. The Director establishes the Institute's objectives, guided by the priorities of the Office of Justice Programs, the U.S. Department of Justice, and the needs of the field. The Institute actively solicits the views of criminal justice and other professionals and researchers to inform its search for the knowledge and tools to guide policy and practice.

Strategic Goals

NIJ has seven strategic goals grouped into three categories:

Creating relevant knowledge and tools

1. Partner with State and local practitioners and policymakers to identify social science research and technology needs.
2. Create scientific, relevant, and reliable knowledge—with a particular emphasis on terrorism, violent crime, drugs and crime, cost-effectiveness, and community-based efforts—to enhance the administration of justice and public safety.
3. Develop affordable and effective tools and technologies to enhance the administration of justice and public safety.

Dissemination

4. Disseminate relevant knowledge and information to practitioners and policymakers in an understandable, timely, and concise manner.
5. Act as an honest broker to identify the information, tools, and technologies that respond to the needs of stakeholders.

Agency management

6. Practice fairness and openness in the research and development process.
7. Ensure professionalism, excellence, accountability, cost-effectiveness, and integrity in the management and conduct of NIJ activities and programs.

Program Areas

In addressing these strategic challenges, the Institute is involved in the following program areas: crime control and prevention, including policing; drugs and crime; justice systems and offender behavior, including corrections; violence and victimization; communications and information technologies; critical incident response; investigative and forensic sciences, including DNA; less-than-lethal technologies; officer protection; education and training technologies; testing and standards; technology assistance to law enforcement and corrections agencies; field testing of promising programs; and international crime control.

In addition to sponsoring research and development and technology assistance, NIJ evaluates programs, policies, and technologies. NIJ communicates its research and evaluation findings through conferences and print and electronic media.

To find out more about the National Institute of Justice, please visit:

http://www.ojp.usdoj.gov/nij

or contact:

National Criminal Justice
 Reference Service
P.O. Box 6000
Rockville, MD 20849–6000
800–851–3420
e-mail: *askncjrs@ncjrs.org*